KURT JOHNSTON
MARK OESTREICHER

::MY FAMILY

MS+FMY
MIDDLE SCHOOL SURVIVAL SERIES

ZONDERVAN®

ZONDERVAN

My Family: Middle School Survival Series
Copyright © 2007 by Kurt Johnston & Mark Oestreicher

Requests for information should be addressed to:
Zondervan, 3900 *Sparks Dr. SE, Grand Rapids, Michigan 49546*

Library of Congress Cataloging-in-Publication Data

Oestreicher, Mark.
     My family / by Mark Oestreicher and Kurt Johnston.
        p. cm. — (Middle school survival series)
     Includes bibliographical references and index.
     ISBN-13: 978-0-310-27430-8 (pbk. : alk. paper)
      1. Middle school students—Religious life—Juvenile literature. 2. Middle school
students—Family relationships—Juvenile literature. 3. Christian life—Juvenile literature. I.
Johnston, Kurt, 1966- II. Title.
     BV4531.3.O383 2006
     248.8'3—dc22   2006024015

Creative Team: Dave Urbanski, Erika Hueneke, Janie Wilkerson, Rich Cairnes, and Mark Novelli
Cover Design: Gearbox

Printed in the United States of America

14 15 16 17 18 19 20 • 22 21 20 19 18 17 16 15 14 13 12 11 10 9 8 7 6 5 4 3 2 1

DEDICATION

This book is dedicated to all the guys in our two middle school small groups.

Marko meets on Wednesday nights with these awesome guys: Matt Holliman, Zach Dierdorff, Brian Brangwynne, Shane Clark, Brandon Maddox, and Aaron Lusteg.

Kurt meets on Wednesday nights with these amazing dudes: Joshua Miller, Brandon Blanchard, Parker Reguero, Ben Lorenz, Jordan Bresler, Austin Mercadante, Ryan Nelson, Scott Phillips, Matthew Overmyer, Dylan Souza, Jeffrey Cohen, Josh Duval, and Troy Hughes.

ACKNOWLEDGMENTS

Marko wants to thank his amazing family—Jeannie, Liesl, and Max—for being so loving and for your patience while I was writing this. And since this book is about family, I also want to thank the family that was patient with me during my middle school years: my mom and dad, and my two cool older sisters. Once again, thanks to the fine people of the Starbucks at Chase and Avocado in El Cajon, for a great writing spot, wi-fi access, and a good stream of strong coffee.

Kurt wants to thank Rachel, Kayla, and Cole—my incredible family—for giving up some of our time together so I could write. I also want to thank two guys named Josh—Josh Miller and Josh Treece—for reading each chapter to make sure this book makes sense to young teenagers. And yes, the people at Starbucks in Rancho Santa Margarita...I'm a wimp, so I don't drink coffee, but you make a delicious vanilla steamer that warms my stomach while I write.

CONTENTS

INTRODUCTION

See this first really dorky photo? That's me, Marko, in middle school. Nice shirt collar, huh? Can you tell just by looking at my picture that I wasn't the most popular kid in school? Uh, yeah.

How about this second groovy shot? That's me, Kurt, in middle school. That haircut *rocked*, huh? Sure, whatever.

We wanted you to see those pictures—as embarrassing as they are—because we want you to know that we remember what it's like to be a middle school student. Partly, we remember because both of us have been working with middle schoolers in churches for a long time. We don't work with high school kids or with any other age group. That's because both of us are convinced of a few things:

- First, that middle schoolers are the coolest people in the world. Really, we'd rather hang out with a group of middle school students than any other age group.

- Next, that God really cares (we mean, *really cares*) about middle school students—about you. And we're convinced that God is stoked about the possibility of having a close relationship with you.

- Finally, that the middle school years (about 11 to 14) are *hugely* important in building a *faith* that will last for your whole life.

What you're holding in your hands is the second book in the brand-new Middle School Survival Series. This second book is all about getting along with your family (duh, that's what the title says!). The first book in the series—if you haven't seen it yet—is about your faith. We have more books planned in the series on friends, changes, future, and school. We hope you'll read them all!

Oh, one more thing: You don't have to read these 75 "chapters" in any particular order. It's not that kind of book. You *can* read them in order if you want (if you're one of those people who likes order), or you can flip through and read whatever catches your attention.

We really believe in you, and we'll be praying for you (really, we will) that while you read this, you'll grow in your understanding (just like the Bible says Jesus did when he was your age) of God and how much he loves you—how he would do anything to let you know him!

Kurt and Marko

FIRST THINGS
FIRST

WHY IS THIS SO HARD?

Being in a family really isn't anything new to you. The truth is, you've been part of a family for a long time...ever since you were born! Our guess is that you're reading this book because things are beginning to change, and you're trying to figure it all out. It's not that these changes are bad; they're just different, which means being part of a family is going to look a little different from now on. Because you're growing and changing, your family is going to change, too. Let us make you three guarantees:

GUARANTEE #1: IT WON'T BE EASY! One of the reasons family life can be such a challenge is that there just aren't any easy answers. Sure, this book is going to give you some stuff to think about and some lessons we've learned, but a good family life really can't be boxed up and sold or written down in a book. The family can be a complicated, confusing thing, and making it work takes...well, it takes work. Lots of middle school students make the mistake of sitting back and expecting everybody else in the family to put in the effort to make it work. Don't make that mistake! God has put you in your family for a reason, and even though it's going to be tough at times, he wants you to play a part in helping your family work.

GUARANTEE #2: YOU CAN MAKE IT! We said it takes work, and it does. But the fact that you're reading this book is proof that you're willing to work at it. You won't be able to change most of the stuff about your family, but you *can* change how you respond to your family and how you handle the challenges of being a middle schooler. There's no such thing as a perfect family. Yours isn't, and ours aren't. But there is such thing as a family filled with members who love each other and who are working together to make it the best it can be! As you start reading this book, it's important to remember that even though you can't control everything that happens in your family, you *can* control how you choose to respond and how you choose to help make your family better. It won't always be easy, but together, you and your family can make it!

GUARANTEE #3: SERIOUSLY, YOU CAN MAKE IT! We just wanted to say that one more time because we know there will be times in middle school when you're going to want to give up on yourself and on your family. Hang in there! God has really good stuff in store for you, and your family is one of the things he is going to use to mold and shape you into the person he wants you to become. You can make it! We'll say it again...you can make it!

WHAT HAS CHANGED?

Big-time change is happening in your family right now! Do you feel it? If you don't yet, you will soon.

There are a bunch of reasons for this—but the biggest reason is that *you* are changing. And when any one person in a family changes, it forces all kinds of change in everyone and everything.

You're changing in all kinds of cool ways right now. But the change that probably has the biggest impact on your family is that you're now on a fast road toward independence, toward being an adult. Sure, you're still a kid in a lot of ways, and your parents still play a *huge* role in your life. You still *really* need them to set boundaries for you and help you make decisions (in addition to needing them to give you a ride to the mall!). But your parents *want* you to start making your own responsible decisions (whether it feels that way or not). They *want* you to get to the point where they can trust you to make good decisions on your own.

But that process of getting from "parents make most of your decisions" to "you make most of your decisions" is a tough and awkward process—both for you, and for your parents.

Add to that the fact that you're going through a wild change in your emotions right now. Most teenagers are on a roller coaster of new emotions—super excitement and flashes of anger and depressed moments when everything in the world seems against you. That's totally normal; in fact, it's good. It's all part of God's great and loving plan to give you more emotions, so you can really experience the awesome life he wants for you.

But that emotional wackiness can be pretty hard on your parents. They probably feel like they don't even know you some days (you probably feel like you don't know yourself some days!).

So your parents (and your siblings, if you have them) are trying to adjust to this "new person" in their home. Sometimes it's great, because you get to start relating to them more like an adult. But sometimes it's really difficult for everyone.

Here's the survival tip—two of them, actually:

First, cut your parents a break. They're trying to figure out how to help you grow up. And it's not very clear sometimes.

Second, keep talking. Your parents need to know what's going on, how you feel, and what you're thinking. Do this when you're not feeling super emotional, and the conversations will go better.

BASIC FAMILY
SURVIVAL TIPS

WHAT IS A "FAMILY," ANYWAY?

You'd think that coming up with a definition of the family would be a no-brainer, wouldn't ya? Believe it or not, there are lots of opinions out there on what, exactly, makes a family a family.

The dictionary defines a family in a couple of ways. One definition in the dictionary is "a social unit living together." The dictionary also calls a family "a primary social group; parents and children." There's lots of talk these days from certain groups about the need to protect the "traditional family" that, in their minds, would mean a mom and dad living together under the same roof with their children. There's certainly nothing wrong with that definition of a family...in fact that's probably the clearest picture of what a family was originally supposed to be, but we all know that if the only definition of a family were "a mom and dad living under the same roof with their children," a whole lot of us would be left out! To be totally honest, it's probably impossible to define family in a way that fits everybody. Because families come in so many shapes and sizes, there really isn't a way to define what a typical family should look like.

But since this book is written to help you survive middle school day-to-day, we're going to define family as the people you live with day-to-day. You may live with your mom and dad and a brother and sister...that's your family. You may live with your dad, stepmother, and stepsister...that's your family. You may live with your aunt and uncle or grandma and grandpa...that's your family. You may split your time between two households...those are your families.

The bottom line is this: All of us live somewhere with someone. The people we live with and share life with day-to-day make up our families. In his wisdom, God has put you in the family you're in, and your family is going to help mold you and shape you into the person God wants you to become.

MY FAMILY IS A MESS!

Take a minute or two to think about your family. One thing you'll notice about your family right away is that it isn't perfect. Nobody holding this book in his or her hands comes from a perfect family. The truth is, some of you feel like your family is a complete mess, and you may be right!

Think about the fact that your family is made up of people of different ages, sexes, personalities, hopes, dreams, fears, likes, and dislikes. Now, add to the mix the fact that you live in the same house, eat your meals together, and share the bathroom. Crazy enough? We're not done yet! Finally, mix in a middle school student (that would be you). When you mix all that stuff up into a family, you've got a recipe for wackiness! Getting all the parts of a family to work together isn't easy...it takes a lot of work by everybody, and some family members probably don't work as hard at it as they could.

We have no idea what your family is like. Our hunch is that you come from an imperfect family with members who are trying (in their own imperfect ways) to provide for you and raise you the best they can. The fact that you're reading this book right now is proof that somebody wants to help you as you wrestle through what it means to be in middle school and in a family at the same time. For most of you, one of your parents bought this book because they recognize that your family isn't perfect, and they want to help you make the most of it.

It would be great if God would just wave his magic wand (or whatever he waves when he does miracles) and make all our families instantly perfect. But he won't. He won't because he wants to use the struggles and challenges of life, including family life, to help us trust him more and to help us become who he wants us to become.

So your family's a mess? Great! Just think of all the room for improvement and all the ways you can help make things better!

WHY YOUR FAMILY NEEDS YOU

You've probably had days when it feels like your family would be better off without you—or at least that things would be easier if you lived somewhere else for two or three or 20 years. If you haven't felt this yet—you will! It's way normal.

So it may surprise you to read these words: Your family *needs* you.

Now hold on: Don't assume we're completely nuts (well, we are nuts, but that's not the point here). Here's the important idea: While *we* might be a bit nuts, God is not. God knows you perfectly—everything about you. And God knows your family. God put you in your family for a reason—and whatever that reason (or reasons) is, it's as much for your family as it is for you.

That *doesn't* mean that God means for bad stuff to happen to you, if your family isn't a safe place for you (there are other chapters about that in this book—see the "Things That Aren't Supposed to Be Part of a Family" section, page 155).

What it *does* mean is that you're needed! Think of all the good stuff you can gain from members of your family: comfort, help, guidance, love, correction, encouragement, laughter, understanding. All those things—you can offer them to your family members as well.

God the Father, Jesus, and the Holy Spirit model this for us. The three-in-one that we call "the Trinity" live in community with each other. All of them have important roles, both in our lives and for each other. And the same can be true in your family.

> "IT'S HARD FOR ME TO BELIEVE THAT MY FAMILY ACTUALLY NEEDS ME. IT DOESN'T FEEL THAT WAY MOST OF THE TIME."
>
> —CARLY, SIXTH GRADE

Here's a survival tip: Live out the fact that your parents and siblings aren't just there for you—you're there for them, also!

TOP SEVEN THINGS THAT MAKE FAMILIES WORK

This is such an important subject that we have a bunch of little chapters on it at the end of the book. But here's a quick summary of the top things that will help make your family great during your wild-and-crazy middle school years:

OPEN COMMUNICATION: So many teenagers start to have a bad relationship with their parents because they stop talking. This is the biggie of all biggies when it comes to having a great family. You have to be committed to talking to your parents about all kinds of stuff.

HONESTY: If you start lying to your parents, you might get pretty good at it. But that will ruin your chances of having a great family through these years.

NOTICING OTHER FAMILY MEMBERS' NEEDS: When you're going through the massive amount of change that all middle schoolers go through, it's pretty easy to always and only think about yourself—your needs, your wants, your stuff. But in a great family, everyone is committed to noticing each other's needs and doing what they can to meet them.

INTEGRITY: This is a big word that you might not understand. We'll explain it more later. But for now, just know that in every great family, all the family members (this includes you!) are committed to doing what they've agreed to do, to saying what they really mean, and to living in truth with each other.

DOING YOUR PART: There's a lot of stuff to be done in every family to keep things moving along smoothly. Lots of jobs around the house. Lots of big things and little things. You can really stress out your family by not doing anything! Or you can really help make your family great by doing your part.

NOT-SO-RANDOM ACTS OF KINDNESS: This is a bit different from the others because the others are all things you might normally think of. But in a great family, everyone surprises each other from time to time, either by helping in an unexpected way or by giving a thoughtful surprise gift of some sort.

CREATING GOOD MEMORIES AND HAVING FUN! Great families have great memories—stories they can tell over and over to remind them of how much they've enjoyed being together. You play a huge role in making these memories.

SECTION 3

PRIVACY

WHY IS PRIVACY A MAJOR ISSUE?

You want your space, don't you? Have you always been that way (some people have), or is that a new thing for you?

Have you had this happen? You're feeling completely ticked at the world. You're so angry that you feel like throwing stuff or hitting something. But— and this really bugs you—you have no idea why. I mean, you could give some lame reasons (teacher wasn't nice at school today, best friend can't come over, blah, blah, blah). But your frustration or anger or whatever this is—it's much stronger than any reason you can come up with. So you want some private space. You know you just have to kind of "work it out." You're also experienced enough to know that if you just go stomping angrily around the house, it will have negative consequences for you with your parents.

Then Mom walks into your room (or whatever room you're in) without knocking and says, "Are you stomping around in here?" Your first response is, "Can't I get *any* privacy around here?"

Or, maybe your family has one bathroom for everyone to share (or at least for the kids to share). And until a year ago or so, it's never been a big deal to you to have your little brother in there while you're in there doing your business. But there's no way that's gonna happen now! And how he bangs on the door and yells, "You *used* to let me in there! Are you doing something *bad*? Should I tell *Mom*?" And he's lucky you can't reach him through the door right now! But you shout back, "Just go away and give me some privacy!"

I'm sure you could write your own story—different room, different circumstances, same result. It's really normal for young teenagers to start wanting more privacy. And it's also pretty normal for your family members to not really understand why you care about privacy so much all of a sudden.

You might want privacy because your body is changing, and you have no great need to show it off! Or you might want privacy because you need a bit of space to think and process stuff, to try to figure out what's going on in your crazy life!

Here's the best tip we can give you here: Have a chat with your parents (when you're *not* feeling emotional—just at a normal time) about your desire and need to have a bit more privacy at times. Explain why you want this—be really honest with them. Then ask them to help set up some guidelines with you for when it's okay to expect privacy and when it's not okay to expect privacy.

MAKING THE MOST OF A SHARED ROOM

If you have your own bedroom, you're one of the lucky ones! For those of you who have to share a room, it may be almost impossible to think of it as a good thing. Before we share a few tips to help make the most of a shared room, let us share our top five reasons why sharing a room is a good thing.

MARKO AND KURT'S OFFICIAL TOP FIVE REASONS WHY SHARING A ROOM IS A GOOD THING!

5. If there really is a boogeyman, there's only a 50/50 chance he'll get you!

4. When your mom asks, "Who made this mess in the room?" you can blame it on your brother or sister.

3. No clean undies? No problem—just "borrow" a pair!

2. Midnight pillow fights!

1. When you get married, you'll already be used to sharing your room with someone who snores and talks while sleeping.

So, you share a room and need some help? Well, you've come to the right place! Here are a few tips to help you make the most of sharing a room:

USE BUNK BEDS. Bunk beds aren't just for little kids! Sleeping in bunk beds is a huge way to save space in your room and make it feel less cramped. Switch spots every couple of months.

TIDY UP. If you share a room, picking up after yourself is super important. Making your brother dig through a pile of your dirty socks to find his toothbrush is no fun (well, it may be fun for you, but not for him). Most conflict in a shared room has to do with mess and not being able to find your own stuff.

CELEBRATE EACH OTHER. You like sports, but your brother likes computers. You like hip-hop, but your sister likes opera. In a shared room, these differences can make things tough...or they can make things really cool! Instead of arguing over decorations, posters, paint colors, and so on, look for ways to combine your unique tastes to make the room reflect both your personalities.

AVOID DRAWING A LINE DOWN THE MIDDLE OF THE ROOM. This is an old, last-resort approach that never works...basically dividing the room right down the middle. The key to sharing a room is to learn to work together to make it a good living arrangement for both of you.

"JUST GIVE ME SOME SPACE!"

You may come from a family that does almost everything together. You eat together, spend Saturday afternoons together, watch TV together...you name it, and your family does it together. Most of the time, this is a really good thing because the more your family does together, the closer you become. The downside to being in a family that spends so much time together is that you may feel like you never have time alone, that you don't get enough "space" for yourself.

Guess what? Your need for a little more space is 100 percent natural! Everybody needs some privacy once in a while. Your parents are beginning to realize that you're growing up and that part of growing up is the need to have some alone time. They realize this, but that doesn't mean they always know what to do about it! So, how do you get a little more privacy and space? Here's a one-word answer: *Timing*! Huh? That's right...timing. A lot of your ability to get a little extra space has to do with *when* you decide you need it. Here are a few examples of good and bad timing:

BAD TIMING: Your relatives are all at your house for Christmas dinner, and you want to be excused early to go read in your room.

GOOD TIMING: It's a normal school night and things are winding down, and you want to go to your room to read.

BAD TIMING: Your little brother needs a hand with his math homework and your mom asks you to help, but you insist that listening to your iPod is more important.

GOOD TIMING: After you help your little brother with his math homework, you ask your mom if it's okay to disappear to listen to your iPod.

BAD TIMING: Your big sister is in her first high school play and the whole family is going to cheer her on, but you want to stay home.

GOOD TIMING: Your big sister is in her 100th high school play and the family is thinking about going, but you want to stay home.

Everybody has the need for a little privacy. A healthy family looks for ways to work together to give everybody the space they need. Your parents are willing to give you more and more privacy, and they'll do it when the timing feels right.

I WAS A MIDDLE SCHOOL DORK!
—KURT

Mike Pace was my best friend. Mike lived down the street, and he had a huge swimming pool in his backyard. In the summer the two of us would spend almost every day in the cool waters of his pool. After a month or so of doing things like cannonballs off the diving board (yes, backyard pools had diving boards back then) and playing Marco Polo, we'd begin to get a little bored. To add some adventure, we'd get more creative—and more dangerous—with our swimming pool adventures. We'd toss patio furniture into the pool and see who could pull it all out the fastest. We'd build bike ramps and jump our BMXs into the deep end. We were doing *Fear Factor* stunts way before our time!

Mike's house was two stories high, and the tip-top of his roof actually formed a peak that was about three stories above his pool. One day we decided it'd be fun to climb to the peak of his roof and jump into the pool. We'd never done it before, but it seemed like a good idea at the time. As soon as we got to the top of his roof, we noticed that in order to clear the concrete around the pool, we'd have to jump out about four feet or so. Mike went first....no problem. I went next...no problem. When we realized how fun and simple this was, we decided to jump off backward the next time. We climbed up to the peak again. Mike went first...no problem. I went next...BIG PROBLEM!

Remember that four feet of concrete we had to clear to land in the water? I simply turned around and stepped off the roof without pushing hard enough to clear the concrete that was waiting three stories below. *Smack!* I landed on my back with half my body in the pool and half my body on the concrete. Mike sat there with a look on his face that said he was sure his buddy was dead. His look of care and concern only lasted about five seconds, though—when he realized I was fine. Then he started laughing uncontrollably. I, meanwhile, was still dangling at the side of the pool wondering what had just happened.

I got up, shook myself off, and tried it again. What a dork!

SECTION 4

RULES

WHY ARE RULES A MAJOR ISSUE?

We (Marko and Kurt) both have daughters in middle school. And we also both have sons who are a few years younger than that. Our daughters are both allowed to use the stove in our kitchens, but our sons aren't. Why is that? Well, it's because we don't want our young sons to burn down the house or hurt themselves. But our daughters are old enough to trust with this responsibility.

Our sons both have bedtimes that are earlier than our daughters, because they're little and still need a lot more sleep.

Our daughters are allowed to go to a movie with friends, assuming we know the friends and approve the movie. But our sons would *not* be allowed to do that, because they're too young.

Our job as parents is to help our kids become totally independent—making all their own decisions for themselves (because they *will* be doing this by the time they're young adults). But it would be terrible for them, and very confusing, if we expected them to make *all* their own decisions at this point in their lives. So we have rules.

Think of rules as "boundaries." Think of a baby cow (no, we're not calling you a cow!). The baby cow needs to know where to find the watering hole and the food. If the boundaries of the cow pasture are too big and the mama cow isn't around, the baby cow would be lost and probably die.

So the trick for parents is to figure out how to give you boundaries that can be moved out and out and out, giving you more freedom and more responsibility when you're ready for it.

But the problem is, you're at a stage in life where you'd probably like the boundaries to be a whole lot wider than your parents think they should be. Some of that is because middle schoolers usually think they can be more responsible than they actually are (sorry, that's not fun to hear, but it's usually true). And some of it is because it's really hard for parents to know how much freedom and responsibility to give you! They don't want you to get hurt, and they don't want you to make choices that will mess up your life.

The best thing you can do is to prove you are responsible with the freedom you *do* have, and be patient. The rules *will* decrease; the boundaries *will* get wider—we promise. Also remember what we've said over and over in this book: Talk to your parents about this, and not when you're mad or feel like fighting.

HOW TO GET RULES CHANGED

Okay, now that we've taken a peek at why rules are such a big deal, let's talk about how to get your parents to change some of 'em! First, it's important to realize that there are some rules that just aren't going to change, and we'll talk about how to handle those in our next hack. But there are some rules that your parents have put in place on a temporary basis that they're more than willing to adjust and even get rid of completely when the time seems right.

When the time seems right is the key! Most parents haven't made a secret list of each rule and the magical age they will free you from it. Instead, they're probably keeping an eye on your attitudes, actions, and behaviors to give them a hint about the best time to loosen up or get rid of certain rules. When the time seems right, they'll make adjustments. While there are probably more than these, here are the two biggies your parents are looking at: *trust* and *responsibility*. You want rules changed? Show your parents you are responsible and can be trusted!

TRUST: Your parents want to know they can trust you—that you'll be where you say you are, that you'll do what you say you'll do, and that you'll honor the current rules. Here's a classic example: When your parents finally let you go to the movies with your friends on a Friday night, they're trusting that you won't sneak into the R-rated movie they've already said you can't see. Honoring that rule gains trust in their eyes and paves the way for more and more freedom. Getting caught breaking that rule results in a loss of trust and most likely the loss of freedom.

RESPONSIBILITY: Responsibility can be summed up in two ways: 1) doing what you're expected to do and 2) admitting when you've messed up. Your parents hope you'll be responsible enough to do what you're expected to do, but they're smart enough to know that you're going to mess up. The way you show responsibility is to mess up less and less, and to admit it more and more when you do! Let's take that same movie example: You sneak into the R-rated movie and get caught. You messed up! But instead of blaming others and saying it wasn't your fault, you choose to own it and admit that you purposely made a bad decision. Believe it or not, even though you've lost a little trust by making the mistake, you've actually gained some back by being responsible enough to admit it!

When you show your parents that they can trust you and that you're becoming more responsible, you'll be surprised at how many rules begin to get loosened up or even changed completely. You may always have to scoop up the dog doo, but you may at least get to choose *when* you do it!

HOW TO LIVE WITH RULES THAT WON'T CHANGE

Every family has certain rules that just aren't going to change. Some of these rules are biggies that probably deserve to never change (biggie rule: At age 12, your parents won't let you sneak out at night, jump into your mom's minivan, and drive six of your closest friends to Canada). You may not agree with all those biggies, but at least they're big and make sense. The big rules that don't change aren't that tough to live with. It's the little rules that are tough to live with...especially when they don't make sense to you and aren't changing anytime soon! So how do you live with rules that won't change? Here are a few things to think about that may help:

STOP COMPARING. Try not to compare your family to your friends' families. Every family has certain things that are important to them, and they may not be the same things that are important to other families. Trust us on this one—parents don't like it when you say, "But (insert friend's name here) doesn't have to (insert stupid rule here)!" Comparing won't get the rule changed, but it *will* make you even more frustrated than you already are!

START SHARING YOUR FEELINGS. Your parents need to know how you feel. Sharing your feelings probably won't get the rule changed, but being open and honest is always the best thing to do. Some of you have absolutely *no* problem telling your parents how you feel, which is great. Just be sure you share your feelings in a respectful way, or else you may be doing chores for the rest of your life!

STOP WHINING! If you play sports, you've probably heard this from your coach. When it comes to rules that aren't going to change, maybe you just need to stop whining. You hate making your bed, but that rule isn't changing? Stop whining! You don't like Sunday dinners at Grandma's? Stop whining!

START BEING THANKFUL! Right now you may be thinking, *Okay, now you've gone too far...the other stuff I can handle, but I'm not about to be thankful for all these never-changing rules!* We're not talking about being thankful for the rules, but just being thankful...period. Being thankful for the good stuff about your family. Being thankful for the fact that your parents care enough about you to give you some guidance and guidelines. It's amazing how choosing to be thankful can change your outlook and attitude toward just about everything...even silly rules that never change!

WHY ARE MY PARENTS SO STRICT?

There must be some special worldwide force, some unbreakable power that causes every middle school student to say, "My parents are *too strict!*" If you haven't said it, you've at least thought it.

If a law was passed stating the perfect amount of strictness, and if every family was forced to obey the strictness law, things might be different. But that's never going to happen, and middle schoolers throughout the rest of time will experience the dreaded "My parents are too strict" feelings. We're going to give you some inside information...stuff your parents don't want you to know but would probably admit if being tortured. This very valuable knowledge will help you understand why they seem so strict:

YOUR PARENTS DON'T KNOW WHAT THEY'RE DOING! You've probably suspected this all along. Your parents don't know what they're doing—they're just doing the best they can. Sure, they've probably read some books and talked to other parents (other parents who don't know what they're doing, either...), but the truth is they're figuring out how to be parents in the middle of doing it. They love you, they want the best for you, but no parent has it totally figured out.

THEIR JOB IS TO PROTECT YOU. A huge part of parents' jobs is to provide protection for their kids. Rules like no running with scissors and no lighting firecrackers in the house are designed to help protect you. Believe it or not, rules like curfew, when you can date, and whom you can hang out with are designed to help protect you, too.

NO **IS THEIR AUTOMATIC RESPONSE.** Because their job is to protect you, parents discovered an all-powerful, super-duper word that seems to solve all the problems of the universe. The word: *NO*! It started the first time you reached for the hot stove. They yelled "NO!" and you stopped. The word *NO* protected you then, and in the minds of parents, it will protect you almost every time. As you've gotten a little older, you've probably noticed "NO" is slowly becoming, "Let us think about it."

> "I KNOW THE RULES MY PARENTS MAKE FOR ME ARE JUST BECAUSE THEY LOVE ME, BUT SOMETIMES THE RULES CAN GET ANNOYING."
> —CAMERON, SEVENTH GRADE

One last piece of inside information—info your parents *do* want you to know: They aren't trying to ruin your life or keep you from growing up. They realize that they can't protect you from everything for the rest of your life. They know part of growing up is learning how to make your own choices. They're just smart enough to know that, for now, they still need to make some of your choices for you.

FAMILY FACT: IN 1966, PRESIDENT LYNDON B. JOHNSON SIGNED A PRESIDENTIAL PROCLAMATION DECLARING THE THIRD SUNDAY OF JUNE AS FATHER'S DAY.

DON'T MY PARENTS REMEMBER WHAT IT'S LIKE TO BE MY AGE?

Short answer: No. Your parents probably don't remember what it was like to be your age. That doesn't mean they don't care. It was just a really long time ago for most of us parents!

Add to that: Most parents really never were your age. Well, of course, they were 11 or 12 or 13 or 14, or whatever age you are. But being those ages today is *very* different from how it was when they were that age. So even if your parents have a great memory of what it was like to be a young teenager, their memories are of a different experience from the one you're having.

Here are some of the things that didn't exist when we (Kurt and Marko) were middle schoolers: cell phones, Internet, cable and satellite TV, Nintendo and Xbox and PlayStations (we had *Pong*, one game!), texting, IMs, MySpace, megaplex movie theaters—even middle schools (we had "junior high schools"—which some of you might still attend).

Add to that: The age at which young teenagers hit puberty has gotten a few years younger over the last 20 years. So you are *physically* different from the way your parents were when they were your age.

How could they remember?

The survival tip here: Don't waste your time with this question. Talk to your parents about the reality of your world and your life, today.

WHY DO MY PARENTS GIVE ME A CURFEW?

When I (Kurt) was younger, my dad used to say, "Nothing good happens after midnight." Oh, but he was wrong. In fact it seemed as if *everything* good happened after midnight! We could go to a midnight movie at the theaters and see an old horror flick. After midnight we could have Denny's almost all to ourselves. After midnight we could toilet paper the house of the cute cheerleader.

Yes, we *could* have done all that stuff, but we never got the chance to because all our parents had a rule about being home before 10 p.m. By the time midnight rolled along, I was usually sound asleep.

Curfews are an interesting thing. Some of you have a set curfew that stays the same while others of you may have two curfews...one for weeknights and one for weekends. It may even be that you don't have an official curfew; your parents just decide when they want you home based on what night it is, where you're going, and who you're going with. In fact, that last one may be the most common. It's usually those three things that your parents look at when deciding your curfew.

WHAT NIGHT IT IS: If it's a school night, your parents are going to want you home early because of things like homework, showers, and making sure you get enough sleep to tackle school the next day.

WHERE YOU'RE GOING: Where you're going has a *lot* to do with how late your parents will set your curfew. Going to a party at church is always going to buy you some extra time!

WHO YOU'RE GOING WITH: This is a biggie! The people you will be with will often have a major impact on how late your parents let you stay out. When you're going to be with your friends and their parents, you probably will be given a later curfew than if you and your friends are going to be alone.

Curfew is one of those rules that probably isn't going away anytime soon. But as you get older, you'll begin to notice it getting later and later. Just remember that it may never be past midnight because nothing good happens after midnight!

WHY DON'T MY PARENTS LET ME SET MY OWN CURFEW?

This is a question that we've been asked a lot, and the conversation usually goes something like this:

Middle schooler: "Hey, if my parents are going to make me have a curfew, why can't they just let me set my own curfew?"

Marko or Kurt: "Dude, if your parents let you set your own curfew, you'd set it for 3 a.m., which really wouldn't be a curfew, now would it?"

In middle school, you begin to experience tension between you and your parents in a way that you probably haven't before. The tension is that you're beginning to feel like you know what's best for you, while your parents still insist *they* know what's best for you. Trying to come up with a fair curfew time is a perfect place for this new tension to show up!

Since your parents, for the most part, do know what's best, they probably won't let you set your own curfew anytime soon. So you should switch your efforts to thinking about how to get your curfew time set a little later. We've discovered that most parents are willing to extend curfew if they think you're ready. Brace yourself, because we're about to give you two tips to get your curfew extended:

TIP #1: QUIT ARGUING ABOUT YOUR CURRENT CURFEW. Every time you argue with your parents about the current curfew, you reinforce their feelings that you aren't ready for more freedom. Before your parents extend your curfew, they want to feel like you're mature enough to handle it. Constantly arguing with them makes them question if you're ready.

TIP #2: GET HOME 15 MINUTES EARLY. Instead of coming home 15 minutes late with an excuse, try coming home 15 minutes early. Walk in the door and say something like, "Hey, Mom and Dad, I'm home. Thanks for letting me go hang out with my friends. Can I help out with anything?" This will totally freak your parents out! And even though it won't result in an instant lengthening of your curfew, it will get them thinking.

WHEN DO I GET TO DATE?

So, why is a chapter on dating in the section on rules? Well, because when the time comes that your parents let you start dating (if you want to, or have the opportunity), rules will probably be a *major* issue!

First, did you read the first chapter in this section called "Why Are Rules Such a Major Issue?" (See page 38.) If you haven't, go back and read it now.

It's hard enough for parents to know how much freedom to give you—how wide to place the boundaries—when it's about music choices and going to a movie with your friends and stuff like that. But it's a whole different deal—a much harder thing—when it comes to dating! That's because there are *so* many ways you can really mess up your life if you make bad choices in this area.

You'll probably want permission to go on a date before your parents are ready to think of you in that way. Or, at least, the first time you ask about going on a date, it will probably be a bit of a shock for them.

Here's our opinion, based more on seeing thousands of young teenagers thinking about this and wanting it: There just aren't too many reasons why it makes sense for you to go on a date with one person when you're 12 or 13. Going to the movies with a group and sitting by someone you think is "cute"—okay, that's not a big deal. But that's very different from going on a date with just one other person.

So our main advice to you is this: Be patient. The time will come. Don't give your parents a reason to really freak out about dating and make the boundaries even tighter!

TECHNOLOGY RULES

Imagine the world without any Internet. Weird, huh? You could never go online to check movie times—you'd have to look in the newspaper or call the theater. E-mail and IM wouldn't exist, and you'd have to send mail, well, through the mail (hand-written or typed on a typewriter).

Imagine a world with no cell phones. Wow! You couldn't call somewhere whenever or wherever you are. If your car broke down, you'd have to walk for help—there'd be no way to call. If you were at the mall with friends and wanted to call home, you'd have to find a pay phone.

Imagine a world with no cable or satellite TV. Huh. Only a few channels to choose from. Or, imagine a world with no gaming systems and no computer games with graphics (only text).

This might sound like a terrifying and foreign world—something out of a movie. But this is the world as it was when your parents (and us, Kurt and Marko) were middle schoolers. A *lot* has changed in the last 30 years, huh?

And here's the deal: While all that technology can have wonderful results (it's nice to be able to use a cell phone and the Internet), it can also bring tons of new problems.

So you might experience *new rules* and conflict with your parents about your Internet use, or how much time you can spend on IM, or how much time you can spend gaming (or what games you can play). Or one of many other possible rules.

There's a reason for these. Too much time staring at a computer screen is really not very good for you! And there really is a bunch of junk out there that your parents want to protect you from (you need to be wise about this stuff whether your parents are strict or not). If you think the rules are too strict, talk to your parents—without emotion or whining. You might not get your way, or you might. And make sure you prove responsible with the freedom they *do* give you when it comes to technology.

SECTION 5

FRIENDS

WHY ARE FRIENDS A MAJOR ISSUE?

It's *way* normal for you to go though big changes in your friends during your young teenage years. And those changes can often bring with them some tension between you and your parents. Want to know why? Read on, our surviving friend!

Put 10 kindergarten boys in a room with a huge box of Legos, and you've got 10 happy kids. Sure, little kids are different from each other—but not *that* different. Their little brains and small amount of life experience keep them more "the same" than "different." But now that your brain has changed in some major ways, and now that you have about a dozen years of life experience, things start to change.

Take music, for example. Kindergarteners pretty much all like the same music. You don't find many metal-head five-year-olds. But young teenagers start to choose friends who like the same things (music being one of them) that they like.

Want to learn a big word? Here it is: *affinity*. That means "alike"—and the deal is: Young teenagers start to choose friends based on affinity (that you like the same things).

But this can cause some tension, both within you (as you struggle with shifting friendships) and between you and your parents (as they struggle with the new friends you're choosing).

We've said this a bunch of times in this book, and we'll keep saying it: This is *normal*. And here's the survival tip: Keep talking to your parents about this. Talking about why you're choosing the friends you're

choosing will not only help your relationship with your parents, but it will also help you think through what kind of friends you want. Remember: Your parents might have some good reasons for being uncomfortable with some friendship choices, because not every friend will be a good thing for you!

WHAT IF MY PARENTS WANT ME TO BE FRIENDS WITH KIDS I DON'T LIKE?

This problem is totally connected with the last chapter (read it first if you haven't yet). Have you had this happen yet? Your mom asks, "Why don't you hang out with Jimmy (or Janie) anymore? He's such a nice boy! (or, She's such a nice girl!)" And you're thinking, *Because Jimmy (or Janie) is a total dork who still acts like a third grader, and if I hang out with him (or her), I'll be considered the biggest loser in the world!*

Or this can happen: Mom says, "I think you should be friends with that nice new girl (or boy) in the youth group." And you're thinking, *But she's (or he's) such a goodie-goodie, and everyone else can't stand her (or him).*

Here are a few thoughts for you to consider:

First, your parents aren't totally clueless, even if it feels that way to you sometimes. They choose their friendships based on affinity, also. And they understand the value of having friendships where you can share in things you both like, as well as the influence good friends can have on you.

Second, your parents want you to have friends who will influence you in a *good* direction, not a *bad* direction (that's often the reason they suggest friends).

Third, your parents will often (not always) be right about being uncomfortable with friends they think will influence you in a *bad* direction. Remember, your parents have a *lot* more life experience than you—they've probably had friends who have influenced them in bad directions, and they've learned from those experiences.

So the survival tip here is pretty much the same as the last chapter: Keep talking to your parents (and not with a whiny, "But, Mom, you just don't understand!" kind of attitude). Talk to them about what you're looking for in a friend. But it's also important to stay open to your parents' input on friends. It's very possible that God could speak to you about your friendships *through* your parents!

SECTION 6

OTHER MAJOR ISSUES

SCHOOL

Your parents probably went to school.

One thing that stinks about being a kid is that your parents always want you to learn from their experiences. If your parents were totally into school and much of their success in life is because of their education, they want you to learn from them and take school seriously. If your parents don't have as much education as they would like to, they want you to learn from them and take school more seriously than they did. Either way, your parents are hoping you'll make the most of your opportunity to learn. Because school probably isn't as important to you as it is to your parents, it can become a major issue in your family.

To you, things like quizzes, projects, homework, spelling tests, and book reports are hassles that get in the way of more important things...like video games, sports, going online, and watching television. School and all the other stuff are going to compete for your time for years to come, and your parents are almost always going to be on the side of school while you will probably always be on the side of the other stuff. So how do you create a "win-win" situation? Here are a few thoughts:

WORK WITH YOUR PARENTS TO CREATE A DAILY SCHEDULE. Each week, look at your homework load, upcoming tests, projects, and so on. Then create a daily schedule that blocks out the times you'll work on school stuff and the times you'll have free to do all the other stuff you want to do.

TAKE ADVANTAGE OF FREE TIME AT SCHOOL. Sometimes your teachers give you a few minutes at the end of class to work on homework. Instead of spending that time shooting spit wads at your friend, use that time wisely so you'll have less schoolwork to do at home.

> "MY PARENTS GET STRESSED OUT WITH HOW LONG I TAKE TO DO MY HOMEWORK, AND I DON'T KNOW WHY."
>
> —WHITNEY, SEVENTH GRADE

GIVE SCHOOL YOUR BEST EFFORT. The difference between a "C" and a "B" really isn't all that much. Usually, it only takes a little extra effort to move your grades up a notch. Your parents probably don't expect straight As, but they do expect you to try your best.

DON'T MAKE IT HARDER ON YOURSELF THAN IT ALREADY IS! There's a lot that makes school tough. One thing that makes it even tougher is when you slack off, get bad grades, get in trouble, and argue with your parents about it.

MUSIC

Music is one of those things that can create all kinds of frustration for many parents and teenagers. There are a bunch of reasons for this—but the biggest one, by far, has to do with a basic fact about music.

First, we need to teach you a word: *subjective.* You know what an opinion is, right? It's a view or thought or "taste" you have that's just yours—not right or wrong—and it could be totally different from someone else's. Things that bring all different kinds of opinions to them are called subjective. For instance, art is really subjective. Whether you *like* a piece of art is your opinion: You might like something someone else hates, or the other way around.

Music is subjective. People have different "tastes" in music (just as some people like broccoli and some don't). And while it's possible that you and your parents could have the same taste in music, it's unlikely. And most people seem to think their taste in music (or art, or whatever) is more right than other different tastes—because when we really like something, we have a hard time understanding why someone else wouldn't.

This difference of opinion (most of us thinking we're "right") can create all kinds of conflict for parents and teenagers.

In addition to that, music is emotional. You know how certain songs make you feel really happy, and other songs make you feel totally pumped up? That's because music connects with our emotions, not just our thoughts.

But here's the funny part of this emotional thing about music: The emotion a song (or a style of music) creates for you can be *totally* different from the emotion it creates for someone else, including your parents.

Of course, we all have the ability to make some pretty stupid choices when it comes to music. So sometimes your parents might have trouble with your music if they think it's bad for you to listen to (like, because it has trashy lyrics). And whether you want to hear this or not, they're probably right.

So here are a couple of survival tips:

- First, listen to your parents about your music choices. If they think a song or a band has lyrics that aren't good for you to listen to, the best choice you can make is to trust them and respect their decision.

- Second, talk about music with your parents. Try to understand why they like the music they like (and don't be a jerk about it!). And try to help them understand why you like the music you like.

CHURCH

If your family is like most Christian families, going to church is something you do together. Going to church is also something you may begin to question your parents about. You've probably already had one of your parents come into your room early on a Sunday morning to wake you up for church, only to hear you say, "Aaaggghhh...do we *have* to go to church today?"

Church is an important part of your family's life for all kinds of reasons. Going to church together helps remind everybody that God is a really important part of your family. Going to church together helps everybody in your family grow a little closer to God. Going to church together helps your family stay connected to other families on the same path.

It's super easy to let the business of life push church out. Your parents are probably fighting hard to keep church a priority for your family because they know that even though going to church doesn't make you a Christian, it's still pretty important.

Because church is such a big deal, it's probably worth talking about with your parents. Your parents need to hear your feedback and feelings about your church experience. Talk to them about what you've learned in youth group. Let them know what's interesting and what's boring. Way too many families go to church together, hop in the car afterward, and drive home without spending any time talking about how it went. Here are a few things you can talk about with your family after church to get the ball rolling:

- Did anybody meet somebody new?

- Did anybody have a good conversation with a friend?

- Did anybody have an embarrassing moment (like falling asleep during the sermon, passing gas, etc.)?

- Did anybody learn something new?

Again, going to church isn't what makes you a Christian. (Quacking like a duck doesn't make you a duck, does it?) But going to church together is a great way for your family to grow closer to each other, to

"IT'S NOT THAT I HATE CHURCH OR ANYTHING, BUT IT BUGS ME THAT I HAVE TO GO EVERY SINGLE WEEK."
—MICHAEL, SIXTH GRADE

other Christians, and to God. Your parents know that someday you'll have to make your own decision about whether or not you're going to go to church. They hope, and we do, too, that going to church will become something you continue to do when you become an adult and have a family of your own.

PHONE, IM, CHAT ROOMS, AND STUFF LIKE THAT

At school you spend eight hours in class with your friends, eating lunch with your friends, and hanging in the halls with your friends. On the way home your mom asks you how your day went, only to hear you mumble a tired, "Okay, I guess," in reply. Then when you get home, one of the first things you want to do is call your friends (the same ones you just spent eight hours with) or go online to track 'em down so you can talk all about how your day went! (By the way, your parents were probably the same way, but grown-ups tend to forget about stuff like that.)

The reason this bugs your parents is because they've done the math, and they don't like how it adds up. Let us explain. You only have 24 hours in a day. Eight of those are spent sleeping, and eight of those are spent at school. That only leaves eight hours for the family to be together. Now, if that's how it really added up, it wouldn't be too bad, but there's more. All the other stuff like sports, homework, clubs, church, and other things like that cut into the eight hours your family has together. Because your parents realize how little time you spend together, they're pretty protective of it when you have some. Because of this, they're probably going to put some sort of limit on how much time you're allowed to spend online or on the phone talking to your friends. They want a little piece of you, too.

You may be thinking, *What's the point? All my family does is eat dinner then sit around watching television or reading. Why can't I just do my own thing?* The point is that everybody in your family has been "doing their own thing" all day long, and it's important to spend a little bit of time together, even if it's just sitting on the couch watching television together.

Look, it's not that your parents don't want you to have friends. They're just old enough and smart enough to know that you don't need to spend hour after hour on the phone or online talking to them. In their minds, conversations about the cutest girl in eighth grade or whether or not your math teacher wears a man-wig can wait until tomorrow at school.

(Psst...wanna know if your math teacher wears a man-wig? Just give it a little tug! You didn't hear it from us.)

TV AND MOVIES

In America, the average home has the TV turned on for almost seven hours a day. America spends almost 10 billion dollars each year at movie theaters. It makes sense, then, that some of the biggest struggles families face have to do with TV and movies! How much TV can you watch? What TV shows are you allowed to watch? How often can you go to the movies? What movies can you rent? Are you allowed to see PG-13 or R-rated movies? Your answers to these questions and your parents' answers to these questions probably don't match up, and that sets the stage for a whole lot of arguing.

Let's break it down. The purpose of TV and movies is to entertain us. Yes, there are educational shows on the History Channel, but we all know you aren't arguing with your parents about whether or not you're allowed to watch *The Life and Times of Benjamin Franklin!* Since TV and movies are about entertainment, your parents are probably going to be pretty picky about how you're allowed to entertain yourself. If they don't like your choice of entertainment, they're going to have something to say about it.

Here's a silly example, but go with us on this one: Juggling chainsaws is a dangerous way to entertain yourself. If that was your idea of fun, your parents would probably do everything they could to stop you. It's true that movies and TV are just entertainment, but there's stuff in a lot of them that isn't real good for you...in fact, some of it is just plain dangerous! The stuff that lots of TV shows and movies talk about and show on the screen is stuff that your parents see as dangerous to you at your age. They aren't trying to keep you in a little bubble, but they are trying to help you make wise decisions about what you watch. And since you don't always make the wisest decisions, they're going to make some of them for you.

No matter how badly you wanted to juggle chainsaws, your parents wouldn't let you. They would make the decision to protect you. Of course, when you got a little older, they would let you make that decision yourself. The same is true with TV and movies...for now, they aren't going to let you watch everything you want to, but as you get older, they will let you make those kinds of choices for yourself.

CHORES

What's up with chores? Think about it for a second: Your parents make you take out the trash, dust the living room, clean the bathroom, fold the laundry, and who knows what else? You do all this, and, if you're lucky, you get a few bucks allowance in return. This is America! Haven't your parents heard of all those child-labor laws that are supposed to protect kids from overwork?

We haven't told you too many of those "When we were your age" stories, but this is probably a good place for one. You wanna talk about chores... let's talk about chores! When we were your age, we knew the real meaning of chores. We mowed the lawn, pulled the weeds, washed the cars, cleaned the garage, raked the leaves, and scooped up the dog poop. Yep, we did all that...and that was only the chores for *one* day! And for allowance? Our "allowance" was dinner that night.

Are we whining? Yes, we're whining! We were whining then when we had to do chores, and we still whine when we have to do chores because chores stink! Your chores stink....our chores stink... all chores stink! But because we're all part of a family and none of our families have a genie in a bottle that does them for us, chores are a part of life.

Being in a family is a lot like being on a team. If only one or two members do all the work and put in all the effort, they're going to get tired and worn out, and the team isn't going to be as strong as it should be. Chores are one of the ways you help your team. Here are three little tips that may help make your chores less painful:

DON'T PUT THEM OFF UNTIL THE LAST MINUTE. Figure out how many chores you have each week, and chip away at them a little at a time.

> "PARENTS ALWAYS SAY YOU'LL BENEFIT FROM CHORES LATER IN LIFE, BUT I SERIOUSLY DOUBT WEED PULLING IS GOING TO HELP ME IN THE FUTURE."
>
> —MARISSA, SEVENTH GRADE

DO A SWITCHEROO. Every now and then, ask someone in your family if they'd like to trade chores for a week. Doing something new instead of the same old stuff makes chores less boring.

SMILE, BABY! Chores stink, and we love to whine about them, but the truth is that choosing to smile our way through them and have a good attitude goes a long way toward making chores less painful. Give it a try!

COURTESY, MANNERS, AND RESPECT

"Please knock before you barge in," "Open the door for your mom," "Don't interrupt while your sister is talking," "Share the remote," "Ask before you use your brother's stuff," "Don't forget to say please and thank you." Sound familiar?

What probably sounds a lot like nagging to you is just your parents' attempts to help you build some good habits. Call 'em whatever you want... being polite, having good manners, showing respect, being courteous...they're all habits most of us could use a little more of.

Pretend for a minute that your family went out to dinner together. In the booth next to you is another family that, at first glance, is a lot like yours. But within a few seconds you begin to notice something. They burp out loud at the table and eagerly try to pass gas as loud as they can (and they're pretty good at it). Without asking, they grab food from each other's plates. When the server comes to check on them, they make fun of her hair and tease her about her uniform. Finally, they get up to leave, and on their way out, they walk past your booth and take a gulp of your soda! Yes, this is a hugely exaggerated example, but it proves a point: Courtesy, manners, respect, and politeness don't seem like a big deal until you meet people who don't have any.

One big reason this stuff is important within your family is because the habits of courtesy, manners, respect, and politeness are a big deal outside your family, too. Have you ever noticed that teachers seem to like the polite kids a little better, and that the players who show more respect to their coach usually get more playing time? As you get older, you'll notice that people who know how to treat others seem have better jobs and make more money. We're not saying this is completely fair; we're just saying that it's the way things seem to work. You're parents know this, too, which is why they make such a big deal about it.

"I LOVE MY FAMILY, BUT SOMETIMES THEY MAKE ME ANGRY.
IN THOSE OCCASIONS, I SEEM TO WANT TO DO THE WRONG THING."

—NAOMI, EIGHTH GRADE

The Bible encourages us to treat others the same way we would like to be treated. Isn't it funny how easy it is to be rude, annoying, and disrespectful to people in your family even though it *totally* bugs you when they are that way to you?! It's not easy, but a good way to develop habits of courtesy, manners, respect, and politeness is to practice treating your family the way you want to be treated.

LANGUAGE

Language can create all kinds of problems between parents and teenagers. And there are a couple of reasons for this—but you've probably already made your parents raise their eyebrows at one point or another with something you've said.

Alert! Alert! We're gonna teach you another big word (you can impress your parents with it later!). Ready? Here it comes: *Fluidity* (say floo-ID-it-tee). Fluidity is a cool way of saying things change. You can imagine something that's fluid (like a river) is constantly changing—that's where the word use comes from.

Language has fluidity. Most people don't think of language that way—because it seems as though our words mean what we think they mean, and that's all there is to it. But if we write the word "cheesy," what does it mean to you? It probably means something that's really stupid, like a dumb joke. But if you time-warped back in history 100 years and said "cheesy," absolutely everyone would *only* think you meant something that was made of cheese, or had lots of cheese on it. Language changes—it's fluid.

The word "gay" probably means three different things to you, your parents, and your grand- parents. To you, it means "stupid" or "weird"; to your parents' generation, gay means "homosexual" (you probably know this meaning also). But to your grandparents (at least back in the day), "gay" *only* meant happy and didn't have *any* other meaning.

So one of the reasons you'll have some conflict with Mom and Dad about your language is that some of the things you say mean different things to them than what you're actually trying to get across.

But that's not the only reason. Most teenagers, while trying to figure out for themselves what's right and what's wrong and where the boundaries actually are, try out saying some stuff they shouldn't say. It's not just about being fluid. You know if words you say just don't belong in your mouth or ear. And if your parents hear you saying words like that, there *should* be conflict!

This is a tough one—because many of your friends will use really bad language, and you'll feel like you need to, too, in order to fit in with them. We don't have room here to go into all the reasons why this is a lame reason for doing anything, but we *will* say that you can improve your family life by being careful with what you say!

I WAS A MIDDLE SCHOOL DORK!
—MARKO

In seventh grade, I got to go on the trip of a lifetime. My dad worked for a missions organization, and he had helped raise the money for the purchase of a new six-seater airplane for his Alaska missions office and was to make the trip north from Detroit (where we lived). A three-day trip, even by plane—and I got to go along!

Did I mention it was January? The temperatures dropped below -50 degrees. One of those days I did what any middle school dork would have done: I lost a snowmobile.

Some nice but maybe-not-so-smart people had loaned me a snowmobile to use for a few days. And I was stupid enough to think I knew how to use it. I'd race off through the woods, out over frozen lakes, having a great time.

Until I, uh, *misplaced* it.

I was gleefully zipping along a wide space between some trees when I saw a fluffy mound of snow ahead. I thought it would be fun to bust through it. Dork alert.

At my moment of anticipation, right when I was expecting a big poof of snow in my face, the snowmobile dropped under me and disappeared. I went tumbling forward onto the packed snow past the drift. No snowmobile in sight.

What looked like a little snowdrift was actually a drift covering up a huge hole in the ground. The nice but maybe-not-so-smart people who loaned me the snowmobile eventually snowshoed into the woods and used ropes to pull it out. They were then smart enough to take the snowmobile back with them.

HONORING YOUR
PARENTS

WHAT'S IT MEAN TO "HONOR"?

You've probably heard somewhere that you're supposed to honor your parents. But you might not be completely clear on what it means to honor.

The word *honor* can actually mean all kinds of things, depending on how it's used. But all the ways to use it connect with the ideas of respect and something special.

So, if someone is introducing the president and says, "It's my great honor to introduce the president," they mean, "Wow—what a special privilege that I get to do *this*!"

If you take an "honors class" in high school, it's a special class that not just anyone can get into.

If something is considered honorable, that means it's worthy of honor, or worthy of respect. It can also mean the person or thing is very honest and truthful. Honorable is actually a title given to judges—the Honorable Betty Judgeperson—and suggests that this person, this judge, is both worthy of respect and will be someone committed to truth.

But to *give* honor to someone means that you're showing them great respect. Actually, you can give honor both to some*one* or to some*thing*. You can give honor to the great sport of, say, trampoline jumping, by talking about what a perfect and wonderful sport it is—worthy of not just your respect, but of everyone's respect.

So to honor a person means, basically, to treat them with great respect.

WHY DOES GOD CARE IF I HONOR MY PARENTS?

With that understanding of what it means to honor (read the last chapter if you haven't already), why does God care if you honor your parents or not?

It's one of the Big 10, you know! One of the Ten Commandments says: "Honor your father and your mother, so that you may live long in the land the LORD your God is giving you" (Exodus 20:12). Why? Why does God care? Some of the *other* commandments—like, "Don't kill people"—are more obvious and make sense on their own most of the time, right?

Stick with us here: God's command that you honor your parents is actually proof of God's love for you. Yeah, we know, that's a bit hard to believe at first pass. Let us unpack it a bit, by stepping back in time to the very *start* of time.

God invented time. God invented everything, including you and us. And God's only reason for making you was because he wanted to love you. He didn't invent you as a neat science trick. He didn't invent you because he was bored. He made you to be loved.

But God invented everything else in all of creation also—and not just *stuff*, but also things you can't touch or own, like relationships and families. God thought up and made it so that a new human would grow inside Mom and be born as a helpless little baby. And God made up the process that says how long it will take for you to grow up into an adult.

The whole time God was inventing all this stuff that impacts you every day, his only motivation (reason) was love, love, and more love.

Bottom line: God knows his invention. And God knows that we need parents in our lives while we're growing up—parents who will nurture us and guide us and set an example for us and set boundaries for us. Your parents aren't perfect (no human is). But they're part of God's loving design for your life, and you need them.

That's why you need to honor them. And when you *do* honor them (show them respect), you're really honoring God.

HOW AM I SUPPOSED TO HONOR MY PARENTS?

Let's go right to the Bible to answer this great question. That "honor your mom and pop" verse is in the Ten Commandments, which is in Exodus (and other places). But there's another famous verse about children and parents that you may have heard: Colossians 3:20. Here it is in two different Bible versions:

> *Children, obey your parents in everything, for this pleases the Lord.* (NIV)

> *Children, do what your parents tell you. This delights the Master no end.* (*The Message*)

It's pretty plain and clear, isn't it? Why should you honor your parents? Well, because it pleases God when you do. It makes God happy!

Now, we're not suggesting that God will zap you with zits if you don't honor your parents or line your pockets with happiness and money if you do. God doesn't work that way. But you *do* have a chance to make God happy—and that's pretty cool!

Remember what we wrote in the last chapter about why God cares about this? (Go back and read it if you didn't already.) It's not that God is insecure and needs you to do what he says, or he'll put you in the corner! God wants you to honor your parents because it pleases him. It pleases him because he knows what's best for you. He knows what's best for you because he invented you. He invented you because he loves you.

So—in the very clear words of *The Message* (the second version of Colossians 3:20 in this chapter)—do what your parents tell you. That's how you honor them. That doesn't mean you can't have discussions with your parents about what boundaries make sense or what rules should be reconsidered. It also doesn't mean that you should ignore stuff that shouldn't be part of a family (see pages 155-163). But it does mean, at the end of the day, that your life will be better if you do what they say.

HOW TO NOT
WASTE YOUR
TIME

NO COMPARING!

Comparing may be the world's biggest waste of time.

Hardly anything good comes as a result of comparing yourself and your family to others. Here's the reason why playing the comparison game sets you up to lose: Because comparing steals your contentment (which is a fancy word for your ability to be happy, satisfied, and joyful with what you've been given).

Here's how wasting your time comparing steals your contentment: You're satisfied with your allowance until you hear that your friend gets twice as much, and you wonder why you don't get more. You're happy that your mom just bought you a new pair of shoes until you notice that the cool kids at school are wearing a different brand, and you hope she'll buy you those. Suddenly you feel cheated and wonder why your life is so tough when everybody else seems to have it so good. Guess what...you've just allowed yourself to be robbed of your contentment! It's super easy to focus on all the stuff you don't like about your family, and this stuff seems to grow even bigger when you compare it to the stuff you *do* like about other families.

The apostle Paul, the guy who wrote most of the New Testament, wrote the book of Philippians while he was in prison. He had been unfairly thrown in prison simply because he was talking about Jesus. He was probably super tempted to compare his life with others'. He could probably look out his jail window and see all kinds of people...people *way* worse than him...walking around completely free. But it was from his prison cell that Paul wrote a famous passage of Scripture:

> *I am not saying this because I am in need, for I have learned to be content whatever the circumstances. I know what it is to be in need, and I know what it is to have plenty. I have learned the secret of being content in any and every situation, whether well fed or hungry, whether living in plenty or in want. I can do everything through him who gives me strength.* (Philippians 4:11-13)

"ALL MY FRIENDS GET TO DO STUFF I DON'T GET TO DO.
IT REALLY BUGS ME."

—PRIA, SIXTH GRADE

Here's one thing you can be sure of: Your family isn't perfect, but God put you in the family he wants you in, so quit wasting your time comparing it to other families.

GOD HAS YOU IN THE RIGHT FAMILY

You get to know the family of a friend, and you think to yourself, *Why couldn't I have been born into a family like that?* Or, *I don't think God knew what he was doing.* Or, *My family is so different from me—I must've been some kind of cosmic mistake!*

Don't waste your time with that. For a few reasons.

First, let's face it, it really is a waste of time—because there's absolutely nothing you can do about being born! You were born when and where you were born, you came from your parents, and that's just a fact of life.

But there's more to it than that.

Remember, the Bible says God knew you *before you were formed in the womb* (see Jeremiah 1:5, which is really talking about the birth of the prophet Jeremiah, but applies to you, too; and see Psalm 139:13). And God is the inventor of the following things that have to do with this: families (did you catch that? God *invented* the idea of family), birth (birth didn't *exist* before God thought it up and made it!), humans, relationships, emotions, the ability to be nice or mean to each other (this is part of what people call "free will"), growth (think of it—God made up the plan for us to be born as helpless little babies, and then to grow up), and the young teenage years. God made all this stuff—everything that put you in the family you're in today.

Here's a really super-important truth: *All* of God's creation is good (God even said that a bunch of times while he was creating stuff—check out Genesis, chapter 1). Sure, we humans can make a big-time mess of God's good creation. But the basic design is great!

If we (Marko and Kurt) drive out of a parking lot straight into another car—completely smashing our own car—the fault isn't with the car's design!

So make the best of the family you have, knowing that God has you where you are for a reason.

DON'T THINK COOLER PARENTS = A BETTER FAMILY

Even though you know it doesn't do a lot of good to play the comparison game, you're probably still tempted to. When it comes to comparing, the easiest place to start is with Mom and Dad.

Almost everybody has one friend who seems to have the "cool" parents. The cool parents are usually a little younger than yours and somehow manage to go out in public with their kids without being a total embarrassment. But it doesn't stop there. The cool parents let their kids stay out later, give them more allowance, give them plenty of space, and are actually fun to be around. They speak your language and even wear your style of clothes. Your parents, on the other hand, look like they just walked out of an issue of *Nerdy Folks* magazine!

The Bible warns us that looks can be deceiving. Just because they look and act cool doesn't make your friend's parents any better than your own. The Bible also reminds us that God isn't impressed by outward appearances—he's more concerned about the heart. Neither of us (Kurt and Marko) had parents who would be considered "cool"...by looking at them anyway. But the truth is, we both grew up with parents who loved us, believed in us, and looked out for us, which is just about the coolest thing any parent can do!

As a young teenager, you're going through a ton of changes right now. This whole middle school thing is new to you, and it's new to your parents, too. They're watching you grow up, change, and become a young adult. In the middle of all this, they're trying to figure

"MY BEST FRIEND'S MOM IS TOTALLY COOL.
I WISH MY MOM WAS LIKE HER."

—DILLON, SIXTH GRADE

out what their new roles in your life look like. Cut 'em some slack! Try not to compare them to other parents. Instead be thankful that God gave you the parents he wants you to have. True, they may not be the coolest people in town, but they're yours, and you're really lucky to have them. (Oh, and guess what? They're lucky to have you, too!)

DON'T THINK MORE "STUFF" = A BETTER FAMILY, EITHER!

There's the family that seems to have the cool parents, and then there's the family that seems to have all the cool "stuff"! In fact, they don't *seem* to have *all* the cool stuff—they really do have all the cool stuff! They live in a bigger house, have a bigger TV, take awesome vacations, and get just about everything they want. Better stuff equals better family, right? Not even close!

If you've never been on a mission trip to another country or visited a church in the inner city, you should. Thousands of middle schoolers from all over the U.S. go on these types of trips every year to help out people who are hurting and needy. These students almost always notice something: Families find a way to be happy even though they don't have much stuff. In fact, lots of students comment that the families they helped actually seemed happier and closer to each other than their own.

Because you see so many people around you with so much, it's super easy to begin to think that your family doesn't match up if it doesn't have the same stuff. After all, isn't it your parents' job to make sure you have everything you *need*? Yep, it is...it's their job to make sure you have everything you need, but not everything you *want*.

When you stop to think about it, you don't really need all that much: A roof over your head, food in your stomach, clothes on your back, and people who love you are about all you need...everything else is a bonus. You may want a bigger house, but you certainly don't need one. Yeah, a bigger TV would be nice, but the fact that your family even *has* a TV means you're wealthier than most people in the world. Sure, a fancy vacation to a tropical island would be sweet, but vacations are just an excuse for families to spend time together, and that can happen anywhere.

> "I KNOW IT MAY SOUND KIND OF WEIRD, BUT MY PARENTS SPOIL ME TOO MUCH, AND IT MAKES ME WANT MORE STUFF."
>
> —ANI, SEVENTH GRADE

If you come from a family that has all the good stuff, don't feel guilty about it. God has given your family the ability to enjoy some of the cool things in life, and that's okay! Just try to remind yourself from time to time that you don't have to have all the "stuff" to have a great family.

All a family really needs is love. If yours has that, it has the right stuff!

SECTION 9

HOW TO GET
WHAT YOU WANT

GETTING WHAT YOU WANT—
WHAT *NOT* TO DO

Between the two of us (Marko and Kurt), we've been working with middle school kids for more than 40 years (combined, that is!). Both of us have worked in churches that are larger than most, and our middle school groups have usually had 100 to 500 kids in them. All that is to say that over the years, we've had pretty good contact with more than 10,000 middle schoolers and their parents.

Why do we bother telling you that? Here's why: We *know* (we've seen it—about 10,000 times!) that you have the ability to get the things you really want in life right now—more freedom, more ability to make your own decisions, more trust. Basically, you would love to be treated like a young adult— and we *know* that's possible. But we also *know* (yup, seen it about 10,000 times!) that most middle school students act in the opposite way necessary to get the freedom they want.

So pretend you're leaning in, and we'll whisper in your ear the secrets we've learned from watching 10,000 middle school students and their parents. Here's how *not* to get what you want:

- Begging and whining is a loser approach. For a few parents, you might change their minds once in a while, but overall, it doesn't work.

- When you're told no, stomping and yelling and getting mad ("You *never* let me do *any-thing*!") will get you nowhere. To be honest, it's almost impossible for us as parents not to bust out laughing when you act that way. You might as well be telling us, "See? I'm still a little kid, and I have no idea how to react other than to pout and stomp!"

- When your parents are trying to decide whether or not to let you do something, and they decide to say yes—be very careful! This is a huge opportunity for you to prove to them that their decision was right, or to prove to them that it was wrong. Think through (and act on) how you can prove to them that they made a great decision!

GETTING WHAT YOU WANT— WHAT *TO* DO

Still leaning in and listening as we whisper the secrets we've learned about how to get the freedom and trust you really want from your parents? (Read the chapter before this one if you haven't.)

First, a little whispered warning: We *know* this next bit is going to sound like we're parents. We are. Remember, we both have middle school girls right now. And we'll both have middle school boys in a few more years. But what we're telling you right now is more about what we've seen over and over and over again with other middle school kids and their parents.

If you want to be treated like a young adult instead of as a little kid...

If you want to make more of your own decisions...

If you want to have more freedom...

Here are some of the things you *need* to do:

- Talk about what you want without begging and without the massive drama of big-time emotion. Talk like a young adult.

- Be responsible with the little bits of freedom you've already been given. If your parents say it's cool to go to your friend's house after school as long as you're home by dinnertime, but you don't come home on time...well, that's what people call "shooting yourself in the foot." You're "teaching" your parents that they *can't* trust you with the little bits of freedom they'd like to give you.

- Do what you say you'll do. This is kind of like the last point, but bigger. Keep your word. As Jesus says, "Let your 'Yes' be 'Yes,' and your 'No,' 'No'" (Matthew 5:37).

"THE BEST THING TO DO IS TO EARN AND KEEP YOUR PARENTS' TRUST. IT'S HARD TO GET AND EASY TO LOSE, BUT TRUST IS THE BASIS OF A RELATIONSHIP."

—AUSTIN, EIGHTH GRADE

- Make good choices. That sounds simpler than it is, huh? But when you show that you're capable of making good decisions, even when it wasn't something that you and your parents had already talked about, they'll realize that you're ready for more freedom and responsibility.

- This one's really hard: Be okay with your parents saying "no". They'll be so impressed that you accepted their decision that they'll be more likely to say "yes" the next time.

SIBLINGS

TRYING TO MEASURE UP

Do you have an older brother or sister? If you do, it's really easy for one of two things to happen—either you're constantly compared to them, making *you* the good kid, or you're constantly compared to them, and you don't quite measure up.

Know what we mean? We've seen this kind of thing over and over again:

- The middle school guy with a star-athlete older brother. The middle schooler tries to make a mark in the same sport, but will never be as good.

- The middle school girl with a super-pretty and popular older sister. The middle school girl spends *tons* of time thinking about how she can be like her older sister, but deep down, she knows she never will be.

- The middle school guy or girl with an older sibling who was a great student. The middle schooler is always trying to meet the expectations of teachers who had his or her older sibling.

See, here's the problem: Comparing ourselves to *anyone* (other than, say, Jesus!) is a total waste of time. The biggest reason it's a waste of time is that we have this annoying (and normal) habit of comparing our worst stuff to their best stuff. And we'll always be the losers when we do that.

Now, you might get some pressure (from your parents, from teachers, and so on) to "be more like" an older brother or sister. And there might be something great about that sibling that would be worth learning from. We're not saying that you shouldn't allow people to influence your life!

"MY OLDER BROTHER IS GREAT AT SCHOOL, AND I FEEL LIKE I'M ALWAYS BEING COMPARED TO HIM. I'M JUST NOT AS SMART AS HIM!"

—CHARLES, SIXTH GRADE

What we're saying is this (Ready? Survival tip coming): Don't waste your time or energy with sibling comparisons.

CAN'T WE ALL JUST GET ALONG?

Whether you have five brothers and sisters, only one, or somewhere in between, the chances are pretty high that it's hard to get along with them from time to time. Okay, chances are that it's hard to get along with them almost all the time!

Guess what? You aren't alone. Did you know the world's first siblings, Cain and Abel, had a real hard time figuring out how to get along? It's true. Cain and Abel were Adam and Eve's sons, and they didn't get along at all. In fact their relationship got so bad that Cain ended up killing his own brother. Now before you get any ideas, please remember that murder is a bad thing and not something you should do to your brother or sister! The lesson: All siblings struggle to get along from time to time.

So how can you get along with your siblings better? Here are a few ideas:

TRY NOT TO COMPETE. In one way or another, you are almost always competing with your siblings. You're competing for attention from the family, for control of the remote, for the last Popsicle, for praise from your parents, and for all sorts of other stuff. This happens so automatically that you probably don't even realize it's happening. Remember, you and your siblings are on the same team! And when you compete with your teammates, somebody always loses. Competing also leads to jealousy, and that always messes up relationships.

TRY NOT TO COMPARE. Be yourself! You may be smarter than your brother, but not as athletic. You may be prettier than your sister but not as popular. You may be a video-game junkie, but your twin may be a sports freak. You may struggle with schoolwork, but your sister gets straight As. Comparing yourself to your siblings only leads to frustration. You aren't supposed to be "just like" your siblings, and they aren't supposed to be just like you!

TRY TO LOVE THEM 100 PERCENT. Nobody said it would be easy, but God gave you and your siblings to each other! They aren't perfect, and neither are you. If the only people who deserved love were perfect people, we'd all be in trouble!

MY LITTLE BROTHER/SISTER IS A BRAT!

So you have a bratty little brother or sister? You've come to the right place! Here are a few common problems and what you can do about them:

PROBLEM: Little brother (or sister) bugs me on purpose.

WHAT TO DO: We recommend the "don't react, respond" strategy. When you're being purposely bugged, the easiest thing to do is to react angrily, tell your parents, or squeeze his little pinhead like a pimple! We don't recommend any of these reactions because they only get you in trouble (the person who reacts to a situation almost *always* gets in more trouble than the person who caused the situation) and let your little sibling know he or she succeeded in bugging you.

Instead of reacting, take a few minutes and then respond. You can respond in all sorts of ways. You can try to talk to them about why what they do bothers you. You can respond by treating them exactly opposite from how they just treated you...shower them with love and goodness when they just flicked a booger at you. When you wait a few minutes before responding instead of reacting instantly, you will almost always handle the situation in a better way.

PROBLEM: Little sister (or brother) acts just like me.

WHAT TO DO: Recognize that the reason your little brother or sister copies you is that he or she looks up to you. It may be hard to believe, but behind all the bugging and booger flicking is a little brother or sister who wants to be like you. Your little brother or sister wants to be like you...that's not such a terrible thing!

PROBLEM: Little brother (or sister) is always telling on me.

WHAT TO DO: Quit doing stupid stuff! Seriously, that may be part of the problem. If your little brother or sister notices you are doing stuff that's harmful or against family rules, he or she may not be telling on you to get you in trouble, but may just be telling on you because there's something going on and he or she thinks your parents can help. Of course, sometimes little brothers and sisters love to tattle for no reason. The best way to handle this is to not handle it at all. Your parents are smart enough to know the difference, and they can figure out how to handle a tattletale.

MY OLDER BROTHER/SISTER TREATS ME LIKE A LITTLE KID!

Older bro or sis keeping you down? We could always encourage a revolt or a mutiny, but those hardly ever work. Plus, we don't want to suggest something that could result in your untimely death. So there must be a better plan.

PLAN #1: Read the chapter just before this one. In that chapter we listed some things younger brothers and sisters do that can drive their older siblings crazy. Don't read any more of this until you read that chapter. Even if you just read it, go read it again. We'll wait here. Okay, now that you're back, do you do any of those things? (Be honest!) If so, you may want to begin to think through how to give your older brother or sister a little space.

PLAN #2: Put yourself in their shoes. No, we don't mean literally put yourself in their shoes because A) they're probably too big, and B) if you're a guy, it would be a little weird to wear your older sister's shoes! *Put yourself in their shoes* is just a saying that means to put yourself in their place, in their situations. If you could put yourself in their shoes, you'd probably see that there are all kinds of reasons they treat you like a little kid:

YOU *ARE* A LITTLE KID! At least in their minds, anyway.

THEY'RE LOOKING OUT FOR YOU. In a way, older siblings view themselves as additional parents who need to help raise you.

THEY'RE THE "FAIRNESS POLICE." Sometimes younger siblings get more freedom and fewer rules than the older ones because Mom and Dad aren't so nervous the second or third time. This *really* ticks off older siblings who often work hard to make sure things are exactly the same for you as they were for them.

> "MY OLDER SISTER IS ALWAYS TREATED SPECIAL AND IS TOTALLY RUDE AND STUBBORN, AND SHE GETS AWAY WITH IT."
>
> —KAITLYNN, SEVENTH GRADE

THEY'RE JUST FOLLOWING ORDERS. Your parents may have told your older brother or sister to look out for you, to make sure you stay out of trouble, and so on. They may feel like they're just doing what your parents want them to do.

These may not be the exact reasons you feel as though your older brother or sister is treating you like a little kid, but they may help you get a little better understanding of why they treat you the way they do.

We'd be willing to bet that deep down, your older brother or sister really does love you and wants to have a good relationship with you. When they do something that bugs you, try not to react too quickly. Instead, try to respond in a way that shows them you're more mature than they think you are!

MY FAMILY

THE OTHER KIDS IN MY HOUSE AREN'T MY BIRTH BROTHERS/SISTERS

Here are some of the sibling combinations we've seen:

- Stepbrothers and sisters. Siblings who *become* your siblings because your birth parents got divorced, or one parent died, and a new parent brought kids into the new family.

- Half brothers and sisters. Born to one of your birth parents and someone else (a stepparent maybe). Half brothers and sisters are often quite a bit younger or quite a bit older than the middle schoolers we've worked with.

- Aunts or uncles (or nieces or nephews or cousins) about the same age as a middle schooler, living in the same home and seeming like siblings.

- Adopted kids and birth kids in the same family as siblings.

And 40 other combinations!

If you're in a family with one of these unique combos, you're *not* alone (whether you have friends in the same situation or not). These kinds of "unique" situations are actually becoming the normal thing!

Here's our advice to you: Any "parents" (birth parents, stepparents, whatever) in your house—treat them with respect, and apply anything we've said in this book about parents to them. *And*, any other kids or teenagers in your house (stepsiblings, half siblings, cousins, other relatives, random kids who just moved in 'cause they like your mom's cooking), treat them with respect, and apply anything we've said about family in this book to them.

"I ABSOLUTELY *ADORE* MY LITTLE SISTER, EVEN THOUGH SHE'S REALLY MY STEPSISTER."

—JULIA, EIGHTH GRADE

Bottom line—whether you're related by blood or not, they're your family. And God calls all of us to love our families.

DIVORCE, STEP-FAMILIES, AND OTHER STUFF

MY FAMILY IS BREAKING APART

Divorce...we wish it never happened, but it does. It happens a lot. It happens a lot, and God hates it. Wow, that sounds pretty strong, doesn't it?! It's true, though—God hates divorce because he hates what it does to his kids. Your parents are his kids, and he hates what it does to them. You are also his kids, and he hates what divorce does to you, too.

Because God loves his kids so much, he hates when we go through stuff that causes hurt, loss, and pain. But it happens. Maybe it has happened to your family. Maybe it's happening to your family right now. Neither of us grew up in a divorced home, and neither of us has been divorced, so we don't know much about it from personal experience. But we've spent a whole lot of time around middle schoolers who have gone through the divorce of their parents, and we've learned some stuff along the way:

DIVORCE IS *NEVER* THE CHILDREN'S FAULT. A lot of times children think they are the reason their parents split up. Or they think they should have somehow been able to keep their parents together. Divorce is always the choice of two adults, and it can never be blamed on you.

OPEN UP; DON'T SHUT DOWN. When you see your parents going through a divorce, it's tempting to sit back and stay silent. You may stay silent because you're angry, or you may stay silent because you don't think it's right to speak your mind. Your parents need to hear your thoughts, and you need to share them! It's okay to be angry, sad, hurt, and disappointed. And it's okay to share those feelings with your parents. If you can't talk to your parents, be sure to talk to someone else you trust like your youth pastor, a close relative, or a family friend. It's even possible that you don't know quite what you're feeling. Even if you don't know exactly how you feel, talking to somebody is a really helpful thing to do.

"MY FAMILY IS BROKEN, BUT WE STILL LOVE EACH OTHER."

—DANYA, SEVENTH GRADE

HONOR YOUR PARENTS EVEN WHEN IT'S TOUGH. You aren't responsible for your parents' divorce, but you are responsible to honor them. God doesn't tell us just to honor our parents when they're perfect; he tells us to honor them, period. You may feel like it's tough to honor them when they've split up, but they're still your parents, and even though it may be tougher now, you still need to try.

LEAN ON GOD. God loves you 100 percent! He doesn't love you any less because your parents got a divorce. He wants to be your best friend and is willing and able to help you face every situation life throws at you.

MY MOM (OR DAD) IS DATING (YUCK—WEIRD!)

We're not exactly sure how or when it'll happen, but if your parents are divorced and single, it's probably going to happen sooner or later. When you find out your mom or dad is beginning to date or has a new "special friend," all kinds of thoughts and feelings are probably going to race through you.

Yuck! Old people like parents aren't supposed to experience puppy love or go on dates, are they? That's kinda gross! It's really awkward and uncomfortable to think about one of your parents beginning to date. Those feelings are natural and okay. It's also natural and okay for your parents to go on a date.

Weird! Seeing your mom or dad going on a date and developing feelings for someone new is definitely going to be weird and even uncomfortable for you. It may help to remember that it probably feels just as weird and uncomfortable for your mom or dad!

Jealousy! You may feel jealous because somebody new is creeping into your family and taking some of your time with your mom or dad away from you. You may feel jealous because your mom or dad is interested in somebody new, and you feel bad for your other parent. You may feel jealous for both reasons. Even though the feelings of jealousy are normal, you want to recognize them and not allow them to mess up your relationship with your mom or dad. The best way to keep jealousy under control is to talk to your mom or dad and let them know how you're feeling.

Why? The longer your parents are divorced, the more likely they'll want to begin dating again at some point. They'll start dating again for the same reason they started dating in the first place and for the same reason you want to start dating: Because they want to spend some extra time with and get a little closer to somebody.

There's lots of stuff about living in a divorced home that you have to deal with that other kids don't. One of the biggies is dealing with a mom or dad who's beginning to date someone new. Just like everything else, this is something worth talking to them about. Let them know what you're feeling and honestly share some of your thoughts.

A NEW STEPPARENT

Since Mom and Dad are probably going to start dating again, it's a good possibility that they're going to get married again someday, too. A new stepparent is such a big deal that it's really hard to fit everything we want to say in one little chapter, but we have to, so here we go! We've listed some of the big stuff about having a stepparent:

WHAT DO I CALL HIM OR HER? Well, you can't just call him "dude," and she probably doesn't want to be called "hey, you." We suggest you start by simply using his or her first name. It's possible you feel close enough to use "Mom" or "Dad," but you certainly don't have to. If you feel pressured to call a stepparent Mom or Dad, talk about it and respectfully share why you aren't comfortable with it.

DO I HAVE TO LIKE HIM OR HER? Uh, no...technically you don't *have* to like anybody. Just like anyone else, there are going to be things about your new stepparent that you don't like, things that bug you. But give 'em a fair chance. Remember, your mom or dad fell in love with this person, and there must be some reason why!

HE/SHE IS SO MUCH DIFFERENT FROM MY REAL MOM/DAD. Yep, of course! No two people are alike, and your new stepparent is going to be a lot different. Instead of seeing the differences as a reason to not like your new stepparent, try to see them as the stuff that makes your new stepparent unique and special.

IS HE OR SHE ALLOWED TO DISCIPLINE ME? That one is a toughie! Your new stepparent will play a part in raising you...and part of raising you is correcting you and disciplining you when it needs to be done. Hopefully your parents will talk this through and come up with a plan that feels like it works best.

WILL IT EVER FEEL NORMAL AGAIN? Maybe...but probably not. Living with a new stepparent is a big deal, and it takes a lot of getting used to. Chances are it will never feel exactly like your original family did, but it can still be really good!

So, what do you do when you have more than two parents, and you live in a blended family? Check out the next two chapters for some ideas!

BALANCING MORE THAN TWO PARENTS

It's tough enough trying to balance all the stuff about being in middle school when you only have two parents. Trying to do it when your parents are divorced and remarried can seem almost impossible. When you were younger, you didn't have much say about how your time was split between your parents, but now that you're older, you're probably being allowed to begin to make some of those decisions for yourself. So how do you do it...how do you balance your time between two families?

COME UP WITH THE BEST SCHEDULE POSSIBLE. Whom do you spend your time with and when? Where do you live on the weekends? Where do you spend the summer? Where do you spend Christmas and Easter? The courts decided some of this, but a lot of it may be up to you and your parents to decide...and it may always be changing. Because life in middle school is so crazy with homework, sports, friends, and so on, it's important that you work with your parents to develop a schedule and rotation that feels fair and allows your life to feel as normal and stable as possible.

CREATE AN "EVERYTHING" BACKPACK. This is just a backpack that has stuff in it that you want to make sure gets taken from one house to the next. Put the book you're reading, your favorite music, your toothbrush, your newest video game, and stuff like that in your "everything" backpack so you don't forget to take important things with you on visits.

KEEP A CALENDAR. One little word can make a big difference! Ask both parents to keep a calendar on the fridge or someplace handy that lists your schedule and other important dates like upcoming birthday parties or tests at school so you don't forget about them.

CELEBRATE THE DIFFERENCES. The two homes you live in and your different parents aren't going to be exactly the same. That can actually be a pretty good thing! Instead of expecting both families to be identical, celebrate and appreciate the differences that make them special.

Balancing more than one parent or family isn't easy. It's full of challenges and obstacles, but we know you're up to the challenge!

HOW TO LIVE IN A BLENDED FAMILY

Blended families come in all kinds of flavors. Maybe your mom married your stepfather, and he has three kids of his own. Or maybe your dad married your stepmother and they just had a new baby together. In a blended family you may have a stepmother, a stepfather, stepbrothers, stepsisters, half brothers, half sisters, and even step-pets! You've got all sorts of stuff mixed into one new, blended family—a family that you are an important part of!

At first, living in a blended family is going to be a really big adjustment. Mixing two families into one isn't an easy thing to do, and it brings lots of challenges. While everybody is getting used to it together, you can count on a few tense moments. But after a while, your blended family will begin to feel more and more comfortable. Here are a few thoughts that may help you along the way:

IT'S A LEARNING TIME FOR EVERYBODY. Try to remember that you aren't the only one trying to figure out how this new family is going to get along and what your role is. The idea of blending two families is also new to your parents, your stepparents, your siblings, and everybody else. Give everybody a little extra grace while you all get used to living together.

IT TAKES TIME. While we really do believe that God wants to help make your blended family work, it's important to know that big adjustments like this don't work automatically. It's going to take a while for everybody to settle in and for things to settle down. Be patient, hang in there, and trust that God has things under control.

DIFFERENT DOESN'T EQUAL TERRIBLE! Your new stepparent and stepsiblings are going to do things that drive you totally crazy. Remember, they're going through a bunch of changes, too. They probably have different rules and family traditions and like to eat at different restaurants. Part of blending two families is *just* that: Blending two families together. This means there will be some changes, but it doesn't mean that all the changes are a terrible thing. In fact, we'd be willing to bet that you'll grow to like some of them.

I WAS A MIDDLE SCHOOL DORK! —KURT

Two little letters sewn onto the pocket of your pants were all it took to show the world you were one of the cool kids. Those letters? OP.

OP stood for Ocean Pacific, the coolest brand of surf and skate clothes any middle schooler had ever laid eyes on. If you were a surfer or a skater—or wanted the girls to think you were a surfer or a skater—you had to wear OP pants. Of course, I didn't have OP pants. It's not that I didn't want them—oh, boy, did I want them! I didn't have OP pants because my parents couldn't afford them. I did, however, have a pair of GW pants. My mom went to the swap meet (a big outdoor garage sale for new, cheap stuff...kinda like a flea market) and bought me a pair of GW pants for about half the price of OP pants. GW pants looked exactly like OP pants. The only difference was that instead of a cool OP sewn on the pocket, there was a big GW. GW stood for Golden Wave, but it might as well have stood for *I'm a loser who can't afford a pair of OP pants!*

I knew I had to wear them to school because my mom was so excited for me. So I came up with a plan. When I got to school, instead of trying to hide the fact that I was wearing GWs, I began showing them off to all my friends, saying that they were the hot new pants and that pretty soon everybody would be trading their OPs in for GWs. I even made up a story that I had read an article about several pro surfers who were beginning to wear GW pants. Since nobody else's parents shopped at the swap meet, the story was actually working! Working, that is, until one of the cutest girls at school called me out. She knew that GWs came from the swap meet and that nobody wore them—nobody, that is, except losers who couldn't afford OP pants.

I felt like a complete dork. And guess what? I didn't feel like a dork for wearing GW pants. In fact, a few kids even came up to me and mentioned that they really liked 'em. I felt like a dork because I lied just to try to look good when I let my embarrassment get to me. I felt like a dork because my mom went out of her way to buy me a pair of pants she thought I'd like (and she could afford), and all I could do was fib my way to coolness.

I went home, told my mom the story, and asked her if she'd buy me another pair!

DUMB THINGS PARENTS SAY (AND WHAT THEY REALLY MEAN)

"DO YOU WANT TO BE GROUNDED FOR THE REST OF YOUR LIFE?"

Why they say it: This saying is usually born out of total frustration on the part of your parents. The fact that they added "for the rest of your life" is a big clue about their frustration level. Most parents will only resort to this extreme threat level for two reasons: First, if you've done the same little thing over and over and over again that they've talked to you about. Things like taking out the trash, sharing the remote control, and picking up your room aren't big deals, but your parents may get overly frustrated when they feel like they're always fighting with you over little stuff. Another time this saying is used is when you have done, or are about to do, something really big and stupid! Stealing, cheating on a test, sneaking in to paint your big brother's room hot pink...that kind of stuff can easily cause a parent to blurt out the dreaded: "Do you want to be grounded for the rest of your life?"

What they really mean: First of all, it's obvious that your parents don't plan to ground you for the rest of your life. This is due to the simple fact that they don't want you living under their roof for the rest of your life! They probably don't even plan to ground you until you're 18, because there are very few crimes that would result in a parent's willingness to lock you up for the next *five years* or so. So, what do they mean when they say, "Do you want to be grounded for the rest of your life?" Here's our translation: "Look, we are super frustrated and disappointed in your decision-making skills right now. We've talked to you about this a whole lot, and it doesn't seem to make a difference. We're surprised that you couldn't come up with a better way to handle the situation or that you thought doing what you did was an okay thing to do. We aren't going to ground you for the rest of your life, but we can't think of anything else to say that will get your attention and let you know how serious we are about this!"

"IT'S SO ANNOYING WHEN MY PARENTS SAY THINGS
THEY DON'T REALLY MEAN."
—SAMANTHA, SIXTH GRADE

That may not be exactly what your parents mean when they say it, but it's pretty close. We know because we've both said it, and that's pretty much what we mean!

"WHAT WERE YOU THINKING?"

Why they say it: This is another saying that pops up when you've done something that makes absolutely no sense to your parents. It is, however, different from, "Do you want to be grounded for the rest of your life," because it isn't only said when you've done something wrong; it may also be said when you've simply done something that makes your parents scratch their heads in wonder. Kurt's parents loved to say this line because Kurt was always doing stuff that just didn't make sense to his parents. He'd dye his hair just for fun, he'd jump off the roof of his apartment, he'd eat an entire box of Twinkies in one sitting, he'd light things on fire, he'd blow things up...the list goes on and on. He didn't really do *bad* stuff; he just did lots of stuff that made his parents ask, "What were you thinking?"

What they really mean: Your parents mean exactly what they just said! They badly want to get inside your little head to figure out what you're thinking when you do some of the odd things middle schoolers do. The reason this qualifies as a stupid thing parents say is because the truth is, most of the time you couldn't give them an answer if you wanted to! Most people don't really know what they're thinking or why they do most of the stuff they do. In fact, most people don't even slow down long enough to think about the stuff they do...they just do it. They may take the time to think about it afterward, but when they do, they probably won't know what they were thinking when they did it in the first place! Sound familiar? Your parents want to know what you were thinking when you piled 12 fire logs into the fireplace or when you shot the world's biggest spit wad at your 65-year-old grandpa. They want to know, and so they ask. But you probably can't tell them. It's not that you *won't* tell them; it's just that you honestly can't tell them what you were thinking because...well, because you probably weren't thinking at all!

Learning to think before you act and to understand why you do some of the stuff you do is an important skill to learn. It takes time, though. In the meantime, be prepared to hear "What were you thinking?" from the mouths of your parents quite a bit.

"WHY CAN'T YOU BE MORE LIKE _____?"

Why they say it: This one really, truly, is a dumb thing for a parent to say! It's dumb because parents should be smart enough to know not to compare you to other people. They should also be smart enough not to suggest that you compare yourself with other siblings, relatives, or friends. But because parents aren't as smart as they should be, they say this from time to time. They usually say it because they don't think you're living up to your potential in some area...in some area that somebody else seems to be really good at. Like most dumb things parents say, they usually say it without thinking and when they're frustrated. For example, your sister is really good at math and enjoys doing her math homework because it comes so easily. You struggle with math and constantly turn in your homework late. In a moment of frustration, one of your parents blurts out, "Why can't you be like your sister?! She gets good grades in math!"

What they really mean: Your parents don't want you to be just like somebody else. They realize you're a one-of-a-kind masterpiece! But there will always be areas they think you can work on and things they think you can improve. Attitudes, school habits, sports skills, and stuff like that have a way of sticking out to your parents when you aren't quite as good in these areas as they think you should be. Sometimes your parents are right... you could improve with a little extra effort. Because your parents want the best for you, they may try to motivate you by comparing you to somebody else. Most of the time this doesn't work because comparing you to somebody else isn't the best form of motivation! Your parents don't want you to be like somebody else, but they do want you to be the very best you that you can be! Part of being the best *you* can be is learning from others. Your parents really aren't trying to discourage you when they compare you to somebody else. They're hoping that the comparison will help you see how much potential you really have.

Be yourself. God made you, and he likes what he made! But don't be afraid to look at others to see what you can learn from them.

"WHEN I WAS YOUR AGE..."

You'll be in the middle of a good, long complaint about something. It sounds something like this:

> *It's just so unfair! I can't believe that they make us do that! I mean, we have to carry all our stuff to every class, because they're too cheap to give us lockers. And we have so much stuff. And my arms feel like they're about to break off sometimes...*

And, at that moment, your dad (or mom) will cut you off with a loud-volume interruption, like this:

> *Well, when I was your age, we didn't even have backpacks, and our books were made out of solid stone, and...*

Or something like that.

Here's a translation of "When I was your age": Stop whining.

That's not a word-for-word translation. It's more what your parents are feeling when they launch that phrase. True, your life might be more difficult than your parents' was when they were your age. But that's not true for most people—at least when it comes to parts of life.

So, yes, most teenagers have it *way* easier than their parents did as teenagers (i.e., rules, TV and other media choices, transportation, and so on). But here's an interesting thing: Teenagers today have other things a lot tougher than their parents did as teenagers—things like stress, too much informa-tion, pressure to buy stuff (from companies marketing right to them), and more.

So, here's the little survival tip: When Mom or Dad starts with, "When I was your age..." just smile, listen, and learn. Think of it as watching something on The History Channel. It's an opportunity to learn something about what life was like for your parents when they were teenagers. Also, take it as a reminder to ask yourself: *Am I being a whining brat right now?* And, of course, make an adjustment in that, if the answer is yes!

SECTION 13

RANDOM QUESTIONS
ABOUT PARENTS
AND FAMILIES

ARE MY PARENTS TRYING TO RUIN MY LIFE?

Short answer: Yes.

No, we're just kidding. It only feels that way sometimes. Maybe you haven't felt it yet—but most young teenagers go through times when it feels like their parents don't understand anything they're trying to say, don't understand the pressures they're under, and just want to make life more difficult for them.

The first thing to remember when things feel this way is that it's *highly* unlikely to be true: Your parents probably *do* understand *at least some* of what you're trying to say; they probably *do* understand *at least some* of the pressure you're under; and they probably *don't* just want to make life more difficult for you.

That might seem obvious in some ways. But when things feel pretty wacky between you and your parents, it's important to start by admitting to yourself that things *probably* aren't quite as bad as they feel. Remember, your feelings are pretty wacky right now, since you're going through such a massive change in how your feelings work right now. And that means you'll often feel things in exaggerated ways (that means, you'll feel things more extreme than they really are).

Here are a few survival tips:

- When you're feeling these extreme emotions (like you either want to cry or start throwing things because you're so frustrated with your parents), get a bit of space to be by yourself. If you're in the middle of a heated conversation with your parents, ask them (without emotion, if possible) if it's okay that you take a few minutes by yourself to think. They'll probably be okay with this. Go to your room and try to quiet yourself down. Try to remember that things probably aren't as bad as they feel at that moment.

"MY PARENTS ARE ALWAYS ACTING WEIRD, AND I DON'T UNDERSTAND IT. HOW AM I SUPPOSED TO DEAL WITH THEIR STRANGE BEHAVIOR?"

—NATHAN, EIGHTH GRADE

- Pray. Ask God to help you understand your parents. Ask God to help your parents understand you. Ask God to help you be calm.

- Try to talk with your parents when you're not raging mad or a weepy mess. Try to talk to them without crazy emotions getting in the way. When you feel the emotions start to surface again, say a silent prayer asking God for help. Stop and take a deep breath (close your eyes for a moment if you have to).

WHAT IF ONE OF MY PARENTS DOESN'T GO TO CHURCH?

There are lots of families where one parent goes to church and the other parent doesn't. You may or may not know other families like this (we admit, it's a lot harder if you don't know other kids who are in your situation).

First, it's important to understand why this is the case in your family. You probably already know—but if you don't, it's a fair question to ask, of both parents. Make sure you ask in a respectful way, not in a way that's mean.

The most common reason is because one parent isn't a Christian or doesn't believe that church is a place for them. If this is the case, there are a couple of things you should be doing...and something you *shouldn't* be doing. Let's start with the thing you shouldn't be doing: Don't nag your parent who doesn't go to church. It's really important that you give him or her space to process spiritual stuff in his or her own time.

And here are a couple of things you *should* be doing:

- Pray for your parent, regularly. Pray that God would change his or her heart. Pray that God would help you to be patient and loving.

- Show how your faith makes a difference in your life. One of the best places for your parent to see that Jesus is real is in your life. Live in such a way that your parent can see Jesus in you. Be loving and respectful.

The two of us (Kurt and Marko) have seen *so* many parents come to Jesus because of their middle school teenage kids! That might not happen in your case, but don't give up hope!

WHAT IF I'M THE ONLY CHRISTIAN IN MY FAMILY?

If this is true of you, we're *so* happy you found this book, or that someone gave it to you!

So, being the only Jesus follower in a family can mean lots of different things. Maybe your family is very open to you being into Jesus, and even supportive. Or, maybe they think it's stupid. Or, maybe they just really don't care. Or even, maybe they don't know!

The first thing we need to say is this: You're not alone, in two ways. You're not alone in that lots of young teenagers are in the same situation. But *way* more important is that Jesus is always with you—so you're *really* not alone! That's important for everyone to understand. But it's super important for someone in your situation.

Here's another important thing to understand: Most of the stuff in this book about how to make your family great still totally applies to you. It would be the coolest, of course, if your parents and siblings shared your faith. But you can still have a great family.

Make sure you talk about faith stuff, but not in a bossy or stuck-up or annoying way. Your family needs to know *why* you believe the stuff you believe. Remember, you can have a *huge* impact on them. But you can also provide a really bad example of what a Jesus follower looks like, if you shove your faith down their throats, or if you don't actually live out what you say you believe.

Your faith needs to make an actual difference in your life! If it does—if you're kind and gentle and respectful, and if you serve them—then you'll give them a great picture of why living for Jesus makes the most sense.

One final thought: It couldn't be more important for you to have a Christian adult who's mentoring you. Find someone—a youth worker, or another adult in your church—whom you can talk to weekly, to help you think through how to act and live out your faith.

WHAT IF I DON'T HAVE A "FAMILY" LIKE OTHER KIDS?

First, we need to say that we've known *so* many young teenagers who don't live with both of their birth parents. We've known kids living with grandparents, aunts or uncles, family friends, adoptive parents, a stepparent, foster parents, and many other kinds of adult guardians.

Then there are all the sibling combos and variations: stepsisters and brothers, half sisters and brothers, and everything else you can imagine. Last week, I (Marko) was talking to a junior high girl who lives with her aunt, who's also her best friend. But get this: Her aunt is two days younger than she! This girl's mom and her grandma had babies (the two girls) two days apart. And now they live together in one home.

If one of the words in those first two paragraphs describes your home, or even if you'd need some other words to explain your not-so-easy-to-explain home, know this: It can still be a home (not just a place to live). And those people you live with? They can still be your family, just as much as a young teenager living with two birth parents has a family.

Sure, you'll probably get tired of explaining your situation to people ("Well, he's not really my dad," or "No, she's not my sister; she's my aunt"). There are worse things in life than having to explain things over and over. But, family is much more than parents giving birth to children and living in the same house with them.

Really, we're not just trying to make things sound better than they are when we say this, but whatever the combo or mixed dish or sushi platter of people living in your house (blood relative or not), they *can* be a great family for you. And they can be just as good, or even better, than any other family (not that it's a competition!).

> "SOMETIMES IT DOESN'T FEEL LIKE MY FAMILY IS NORMAL, BECAUSE WE'RE NOT LIKE OTHER FAMILIES."
> —CELESTE, SIXTH GRADE

All the stuff we're saying in all the other chapters in this book—it *all* still applies to you and your unique family. Okay? Got it?

WHAT AM I SUPPOSED TO DO IF MY PARENTS DON'T GET ALONG?

This is a tough one. And it's so much more common than you might think.

First, let's get this out there: *All* human relationships have conflict (disagreements, fights, hurt feelings, and so on) at times, because *all humans* sin. The only relationships that never have had and never *will* have conflict are the relationships between God the Father, Jesus, and the Holy Spirit—because their relationship isn't messed up by sin. So, it's totally normal that your parents have relational rough spots—every marriage does.

But you might live in a home where your parents are way beyond the once-in-a-great-while disagreement or fight. Maybe they fight all the time. Maybe they hardly agree on anything. Maybe they say mean things about each other to you. Maybe they hardly even talk to each other, or even sleep in different rooms (and really lead separate lives).

This book isn't about your parents and their problems. It's also not a book about how to "fix" your parents. This is a book about you, as an important part of your family. So we're going to talk a little about what you *can* and *should* do if you're in this kind of situation.

We need to tell you that living in a home where your parents are always fighting (or not even talking) is one of the hardest things a child or teenager will ever have to do. And any "helpful" response on your part calls for a certain level of grown-up-ness, or maturity. It won't be easy.

It's super important that you remember to show love to both parents. Treat them both with respect. And, unless one of them is hurting you (with words or physically), try not to take sides. If you take sides, you could actually make the situation worse—and you don't want that!

One of the things we've seen happen a lot in these kinds of situations is that the parents can (accidentally or on purpose) get you caught in the middle, and try to use you to get back at the other parent. Don't allow yourself to get caught in the middle like this. Tell them both that you love them, but that you don't want to be caught in the middle. This might be hard for them to hear, but it's important for your survival.

It's also important that, in situations like these, you have some other adult to talk to. Find a trusted youth worker or school counselor or someone (who's not involved in the problem) you can talk to regularly about the problem and about your response.

THINGS THAT AREN'T SUPPOSED TO BE PART OF A FAMILY

ABUSE

We've talked a lot in this little book about the fact that there is no such thing as the perfect family. Even though every family has its share of junk, there is some stuff that should *never* be part of *any* family.

Abuse: One simple definition of abuse is purposely treating someone else in a harmful way. You'd think that the family should be a place that protects each other from abuse, but sadly, a whole lot of the abuse that takes place happens inside the family. Here are some examples of abuse:

- Sexual abuse: This is when somebody purposefully mistreats another family member in a sexual way. Inappropriate kissing, sexual talk, and sexually touching another family member are very dangerous types of abuse.

- Physical abuse: This is when a family member hits, punches, kicks, or uses other forms of physical punishment. We aren't talking about a parent spanking a child for disobeying...that's not abuse. What we're talking about is physical punishment that's meant to cause harm and is done out of anger.

- Verbal abuse: That old saying that says, *Sticks and stones may break my bones, but words will never hurt me,* is cute, but it's just not true! Words are very powerful and are often used as a type of abuse. Verbal abuse happens when a family member uses harsh, improper, discouraging words to hurt another member of the family on purpose.

God knows your family isn't perfect. But despite all the problems your family has, he still expects the family to love each other, protect each other, and look out for each other. We'll talk a little later about what to do if there is abuse in your family. But for now just remember that there are lots of little things about your family that keep it from being perfect. Abuse isn't one of those little things! Abuse is a big thing...in fact, it's a huge thing.

MY FAMILY

RAGE

Some people think that getting mad is a sin and that good Christians should never get upset. Not only do Christians get mad, but Jesus Christ himself got mad! Jesus was visiting a temple (a Jewish church) one day and noticed that there were tons of people selling things and using it like a marketplace. It was like a big flea market or swap meet. The Bible says that Jesus got so upset that he ran everybody off the property. Jesus was angry, but he didn't sin. God knows that things happen that cause us to be angry and that sometimes anger is the right response to a situation. He just doesn't want our anger to turn into something bigger than it needs to be. When it does, it becomes a sin.

Rage is an example of anger that has become sin. Rage is basically anger that has become extreme, violent, or out of control. It's when somebody gets so mad that they just can't control what they're saying and doing. In a family, there will be plenty of things that make people upset and angry. But rage should never be a normal part of your family. For sure, there will be times when somebody in your family lets their anger go too far and slip into rage...that happens even though it shouldn't. What you want to be aware of is that if rage becomes a normal part of your family life, it can do a lot of damage!

The biggest reason rage doesn't belong in a family is that it's the leading cause of two of the three types of abuse we talked about in the last chapter. Physical and verbal abuse are almost always the result of rage. Think about it: Parents or brothers and sisters would hardly ever do or say something on purpose that they know is harming somebody in their family...but when they're super angry and out of control, their rage causes them to cause physical and verbal harm. That's why people are super apologetic for their actions after they cool down and realize that their rage resulted in physical or verbal abuse. They will even say things like, "I love you and would never purposely do that to you." They're right, they wouldn't do something like that on purpose, but their rage caused them to lose control.

Because the family is supposed to be a place of encouragement, protection, and support, rage can't be part of a healthy family.

NEGLECT

Neglect probably isn't a word you hear very often. A basic definition of neglect is to give little or no attention to something. When you don't do your chores, you have neglected them. When you don't do your homework, you have neglected it. When you pretend you can't hear your little brother hollering from the bathroom for a new roll of toilet paper, you have neglected him! Those are little examples of neglect and are part of any normal family. But there is a bigger type of neglect that we want to talk about...a type of neglect that doesn't happen a lot, but when it does, it goes against everything the family is supposed to be about.

The Bible says, "If anyone does not provide for his relatives, and especially for his immediate family, he has denied the faith and is worse than an unbeliever" (1 Timothy 5:8). The family is supposed to take care of each other and help meet each other's needs. The Bible doesn't say that your parents are supposed to make sure you have everything you *want*; it says they are supposed to make sure you have everything you *need*. When family members are purposely giving little or no attention to the things other family members need, they are neglecting them.

You definitely need some stuff from your parents. You need food, clothing, shelter, love, support, attention, protection, and encouragement. When parents purposely ignore this stuff, they are neglecting their child and are causing all kinds of harm to the family. God expects your parents to provide all this stuff for you. You need food, but you don't need to eat at fancy restaurants all the time. You need clothing, but you don't need name-brand jeans that cost $100. You need shelter, but you don't need to live in a fancy house in the best part of town.

God has given your family to each other. He hopes the family will be a place where you receive the things you need. Look back at the last paragraph. There aren't a *ton* of things you really need from your family, but the things do you need are *super* important. It's important to God that the family doesn't neglect to provide these things for each other.

WHAT TO DO ABOUT THIS STUFF

We sure wish we didn't have to write this chapter, but we know that for some of you, this little chapter may be the most important one in the whole book. Abuse, rage, and neglect...none of this stuff should be part of your family. But what do you do if it is? Lots of people think that the bigger the problem is in a family, the more the family should work to keep it a secret so nobody finds out. But the truth is that the bigger the problems, the bigger the need for your family to get some help. Some problems are just too big and too important to keep a secret or to try to work out on your own. Abuse, rage, and neglect are three of these types of problems. Some family secrets are worth keeping. The secret that your mom dyes her hair to hide the gray or that your dad sucks in his stomach when he looks in the mirror are probably okay to keep in the family! Abuse, rage, and neglect should *never* be kept a secret...no matter what your parents may say. So what do you do?

Talk to somebody! If a brother or sister is responsible for the problem, be sure to talk to your parents. They may not realize that some of this stuff is happening, and they need to know. If it's just one of your parents responsible for the problem, talk to your other parent. Sometimes one parent will abuse family members without the other parent knowing it's happening.

Talk to somebody else! Like we mentioned before, sometimes families think it's best to hide the big problems like abuse, rage, and neglect, or to try to handle it on their own. Sometimes parents will make excuses for why it's happening or try to convince their children that they're making a big deal out of nothing. If you talk to your parents and nothing seems to get better, it's time to talk to somebody else. A trusted family friend, an aunt or uncle, a pastor, or even a police officer are all people you can talk to if abuse, rage, or neglect is happening in your family. Think of somebody you trust who would be willing to help, and talk to them about what's going on.

Remember, getting help sounds tough, but it's important! Lots of people never ask for the help they need because they're scared, embarrassed, or nervous about what will happen if they share what's going on in their family. When people don't ask for help, they get stuck in a dangerous family situation. God wants to help your family work...but sometimes he uses the help of other people. And other people can't help unless you tell them what's going on.

A FEW BIBLICAL
FAMILIES TO
LEARN FROM

SAUL AND JONATHAN

Saul was the king, and Jonathan was one of his sons. Saul was a complicated guy. For much of his life, he really wanted to live for God. But he had so much gunky stuff in his heart—so many things that messed him up in a major way.

A couple of Saul's biggest issues were his need to have more and more and more power and his uncontrollable jealousy. These two things ended up making him a super-insecure man—always wondering if people were trying to take away his power or if people were getting things he didn't get (which would make him jealous). These issues ended up ruining Saul.

Jonathan, on the other hand, didn't have those issues at all. From all we know of Jonathan, he was a really good kid—very loyal, friendly, and caring. (You can read all about their stories in 1 Samuel.)

The big challenge for Jonathan came when his dad wanted to kill his best friend, David (uh, we're sure that would be a problem for most teenagers!). Saul was super jealous of David because David had already been chosen as the next king, and people seemed to like him a whole lot better.

Here's a tough truth: You're old enough now to be responsible for yourself. You can't just hide behind, "My parents told me to do this." Jonathan understood this: He couldn't just stand by and let his dad kill David. He knew that was wrong, and he knew that if he didn't do anything, he would be doing wrong. But he was also committed to being respectful to his dad. Not an easy thing to do in a situation like that!

Hopefully, you won't get in situations like Jonathan's. But there could come a time when you have to stand up for what's right, even if it's not what your parents want. And the really, really tough thing in a time like that is to not be a complete jerk to your parents—to still treat them with respect.

The survival tip is found in this: Everyone on earth is a sinner; we *all* make really bad choices at times—including your parents. If you can hold on, in these times, to the fact that your parents (or parent) aren't perfect people, just like all of us, you can still care about and love them. And you can ask God to give you understanding of how you can make the right choice while still showing love to your parents.

DAVID AND ABSALOM

King David was quite a guy—the Bible tells us he loved God with *all* his heart. But he was a messy guy. He made some *huge* mistakes and bad choices—with some *huge* consequences!

Absalom was one of David's sons. And Absalom was a *major* mess! In fact, Absalom had two constant focuses that ended up killing him. First, he was really stuck-up. He was constantly focused on his own beauty. He had big-time Hollywood hair (seriously!) and *loved* how sweet his long hair was (can you picture him standing in front of a mirror, combing his hair and smiling?). Absalom's other big issue was jealousy of his dad. He was always bugged by everything his dad did. And this jealousy became such a huge part of Absalom that he couldn't quite live without it.

Get this: Absalom tried to kill his father, more than once, because he was jealous of him.

Here's something you can learn from Absalom: Jealousy never gets you anywhere good, even if it's jealousy for what your parents have. If your mom or dad *have* stuff or *get to do* stuff that you don't get (but wish you did), it's a complete waste of time to be jealous. And while the consequences of your jealousy may not be as extreme as Absalom's (his hair got caught in a tree while he was chasing David on a mule!), any jealousy you have toward your parents will end up ruining your relationship with them. And it could ruin your life. Don't go there!

JESUS AND HIS PARENTS

You've probably heard the story of Jesus, when he was just about your age, hanging out in the temple (the main place of worship for Jews in Jerusalem) and freaking out his parents. Just about everyone who reads or hears that story tightens up shoulder muscles and feels the pain of the situation. Parents feel the frustration of Jesus' parents, and teenagers feel Jesus' frustration, thinking, *I would be in so much trouble if I did that!*

Real quick, in case you're not familiar with the story: Jesus' family took this minor trek to Jerusalem for a big-time Jewish religious holiday (kind of like going to Grandma's house, two or three days away, for Easter)—except in this case, the location was the whole point. Jerusalem was considered the most holy place for all Jews—so much so that God actually lived in the part of the temple called "the holy of holies."

Anyhow, young Jesus was somewhere in the process of learning and growing, just like you are. It's not clear to us, but he was probably just starting to fully understand who he was—the Son of God and all that! The temple had some of the wisest and smartest rabbis (Jewish teachers, kind of like our pastors and ministers). Jesus somehow wandered off from his parents and got into a multi-day conversation about God-stuff with a group of rabbis. All this while his parents and their traveling companions were headed home, thinking Jesus was with them.

When his parents found out he wasn't with them, they rushed back to Jerusalem and found him. His mom laid into him: "Why would you do that to us?!" To which Jesus gave the answer that causes the flinch we talked about. He says, calmly, "Why would you be looking for me anywhere else? Didn't you know I would be in my Father's house?"

Okay, so, yeah, God is his real Father and all. But, *wow*! Duuuude! Harsh!

Here's something we can learn from this: Even Jesus got frustrated with his parents! And even the parents of Jesus got frustrated with him! So, really, if the God of the universe (that would be Jesus) got frustrated with his parents, maybe it shouldn't surprise you that you will also. And if the earthly parents of *Jesus* got frustrated with him, well, of *course* your parents will with you. Just remember: Keep talking, honor, respect, forgive.

JACOB AND ESAU

Got siblings? Do they make you angry sometimes?

Here's a fact of life: If your answer to the first question is yes (I have siblings), then the answer to the second question is *always*, for *everyone*, pretty much without exception, a strong and loud and quick YES!

All siblings have conflict sometimes (or, for some, all the time). It's normal: You're human, around the same age, and sharing some of the same space. But, hopefully, you've never pulled a Jacob and completely changed the life of your sibling, forever.

Jacob and Esau (say EE-saw) were brothers, sons of Isaac (say EYE-zick). Esau was the older brother, and he was a big-time manly man. Strong and hairy, he loved to hunt and grunt and all kinds of tough things. Jacob, on the other hand, liked staying around home more. He was kind of artsy and much more gentle.

Back then, there was a practice called a "birthright." The oldest son in a family got a *much* larger portion of the father's stuff (money, cows, stuff like that) when the father died. It might not sound fair to you, but it was normal back then. Jacob wasn't too happy about Esau having the birthright. So when his dad was really old and about to die, he did something really awful. He put together a fancy trick to fool his father and steal his father's blessing from Esau. (You can read the whole messy story in Genesis 27.)

Jacob's little mean trick ruined his relationship with his brother forever—they became enemies. And it didn't do much to help Jacob's relationship with his dad, either!

Here's something you can learn from Jacob: There will be plenty of times during your teenage years when you can lie, or act, or not tell the whole truth in order to get a sibling in trouble (just to be mean), or to get something for yourself (that should have belonged to your brother or sister), or just to make yourself look better and make your brother or sister look bad. But it's not worth it. A good and strong relationship with your siblings should last for a lifetime and will be super important to you as you grow older. Don't be a Jacob: Don't lie to get things you want now, only to give up a really important and valuable relationship with your sibling!

RUTH AND NAOMI

If you watch enough TV shows, see enough movies, or listen to enough jokes, you'll notice that one family member always seems to get picked on the most: The mother-in-law! When a person grows up and gets married, the mother of the person he or she married becomes the mother-in-law. Now, instead of one mom, you suddenly have two! Hollywood loves to poke fun at the mother-in-law, and so do most married people.

Ruth had a mother-in-law named Naomi (say nay-OH-me). Ruth had married Naomi's son, but something terrible happened. Within a short period of time, both of their husbands died. Left without their husbands, it would have been perfectly normal to think that Ruth and Naomi would simply go their separate ways. In fact, since Ruth was still pretty young, Naomi encouraged her to move back home and try to find a new husband to take care of her. You'd think that Ruth would be running for the hills saying something like, "I'm sad my husband is dead, but at least I can finally get away from his mom!" It would make sense that Ruth would head home and start a new life.

But there must have been something different about their relationship. Ruth loved Naomi and insisted on keeping what was left of their family together. She refused to move home and stayed with Naomi even though that made it almost certain she would never get married and start a new family again. She was wrong! While living with Naomi, Ruth met a rich man named Boaz, whom she ended up marrying, and he made sure Ruth's mother-in-law, Naomi, was also taken care of.

What's the point? When unexpected things happen in your family, you need to stick together! God always has a plan for your family...even when tough times hit and you don't know what's next.

To read the entire story of Ruth and Naomi, open up your Bible to the book of Ruth in the Old Testament. Wow, she's such an incredible family member that she even got a book of the Bible named after her!

JOE'S BROS

Jacob had 12 sons, but the Bible says that Joseph was his favorite. To show how much he loved Joseph, his dad made him a really fancy, colorful robe. This gift made Joseph's brothers so jealous that they were filled with hatred for him. In fact, the hatred and jealousy got so bad that they decided to do something about it. One day while they were all out in the desert, they saw a caravan of people wandering by and simply sold Joseph to them as a slave. That's right—Joseph's own brothers sold him into slavery! His brothers tore his robe from him, killed an animal, and smeared the blood all over Joseph's robe. Then they went home and told their dad that Joseph had been attacked and killed by a wild animal. End of story? Not even close!

The people who bought Joseph were going to Egypt. When they got there, they sold Joseph to a guy named Potiphar who was a high-ranking assistant to Pharaoh, the ruler of the entire country! Over the next several years, all kinds of crazy stuff happened to Joseph, but he stayed close to God and refused to become bitter and angry. Throughout all this stuff, Pharaoh noticed that Joseph was an honest man he could trust, so he made him second in command. Joseph, the boy who was sold as a slave, had become the second most powerful man in the entire country of Egypt!

Years later, the land was struck by a terrible famine, which means there was a really bad shortage of food. Lots of families were coming to visit Pharaoh in Egypt to ask for help. One of those families was Joseph's. Joseph's dad, Jacob, had sent his sons to Egypt to ask for food to survive the famine. As it turns out, the person they had to talk to for help was Joseph! Time for some sweet revenge! But that's not what happened. Instead, Joseph forgave his brothers for what they had done and invited all of them and their families to move to Egypt to live with him.

So what's the point? The point is that forgiveness is a powerful thing! And it's something you will need to give to your family members quite a few times.

Joseph's story is one of the best in the whole Bible. It's a long one, but a good one. You can find his whole story in the book of Genesis, chapters 37–50.

THE PRODIGAL SON'S FAMILY

You've probably heard this one before...the story Jesus told about the son who took his inheritance early and hit the road for a life of luxury and parties. You probably know that when he ran out of money, he decided to return home. His plan was to ask his dad if he could be one of the servants because he didn't deserve to be his son anymore. You also probably know how the story ends. When the dad saw his son in the distance, he ran out to meet him and ordered the servants to plan a massive party to celebrate! His dad totally forgave him and welcomed him back home. Unfortunately, not everybody in the story was glad he was home. His older brother couldn't figure out why his dad was so happy. After all, his brother had grabbed his inheritance, left the family business, and took off on his own, only to waste all the money on girls and partying! Why would his dad welcome him back? Why would his dad throw him a welcome-home party when he really deserved some sort of punishment?

So what's the point? Well, in this story there are a whole bunch of points. We'll just list a few for you:

FAMILIES FORGIVE. Forgiveness was the main theme in Joseph's story, and here it is again! Maybe that's because your family is going to have lots of chances to forgive each other.

THE RIGHT THING TO DO DOESN'T ALWAYS SEEM FAIR. It didn't seem fair to the older brother that he had been a good son and his dad never seemed to notice. But his brother acted like an idiot, and his dad threw him a party! The dad knew that celebrating the return of his son was the right thing to do, even if it didn't seem fair. When it comes to stuff in your family, your parents are going to try to do what they think is right. Sometimes it will seem fair, and sometimes it won't.

HOW YOU RESPOND IS UP TO YOU. Your brother doesn't get put on restriction even though you think he should have. Your sister is allowed to stay out later than you are. When stuff happens that doesn't seem fair, you have a choice to make. You can grumble and complain, or you can trust that your parents are doing the best they can and making decisions they feel are the best for you.

To read the entire story of the prodigal son, check out the book of Luke, chapter 15.

I WAS A MIDDLE SCHOOL DORK!
—MARKO

I'd been acting silly in class for a few weeks and had gotten in trouble a few times. My teacher liked to assign "timers" (that's what she called them) as a consequence. These were mind-numbing assignments of writing a sentence a certain number of times.

I had to write, "I will be quiet and pay attention in class," a hundred times. Then, a few days later, I had to write it 500 times. That time actually took some work at home, in my bedroom.

But the third time it happened, my teacher was really ticked. She assigned me the same sentence 10,000 times. It was a Friday, and she told me it had to be turned in first thing Monday morning. Have you ever tried to write something 10,000 times? It's a lot of times! And it takes a really long time!

Well, I knew I would be in so much trouble if my parents found out. So I lied to them. I told them I had a secret project to work on in my room and got to work. After working on it Friday night and most of the day Saturday, I still had a long way to go. My parents kept asking me questions about my "secret project," and I kept making up new lies and pretending to be excited about it.

But eventually I realized two things: First, unless I stayed up way past my bedtime and worked on it all day Sunday (which would have pushed my parents past curious into demanding to know what

I was doing), I would never finish. And second, I was trapped in my lies because I wasn't going to have anything to show them as the result of my "secret project."

So, in tears, I confessed the whole thing. Yup. I got further consequences from my parents. And I had to stay up crazy-late Saturday and Sunday nights and write all day Sunday to finish.

I will be quiet and pay attention in class.

I will be quiet and pay attention in class.

I will be quiet and pay attention in class.

KEYS TO KEEPING THINGS GOOD IN YOUR FAMILY

OPEN COMMUNICATION

This is the most important chapter in this whole book! Seriously. At least, if you want to have a great life with your family through your teenage years— which is not an easy or simple thing to do—then this is the most important.

Here's the dealio: You're changing, and your parents are trying to adjust to that change. It's a tricky little dance, and sometimes you'll step on each other's toes!

In the middle of all that changing and adjusting, communication (talking to each other, especially about important stuff) often gets difficult. And *so* many teenagers and parents just give up and stop communicating. Let us give you a couple of examples.

You come home from school feeling lousy. You don't really know why. Your mom asks you—in a way that bugs you, but you don't know why it bugs you—why you seem so "down." You try to put words to it, but you don't have the words. Mom gets frustrated because she thinks you won't tell her what's going on in your life. You get frustrated because Mom keeps bugging you about it. And you both learn to just stay away from talking about why you seem "down"—because it's not fun for either of you.

Or you really want to go to your friend's house, but your homework for the weekend isn't done. You try to explain why it will be no problem to finish the homework on Saturday. But your parents aren't budging—they want you to finish it before you go anywhere. You get upset and they get upset, and none of you is really listening to each other. You yell, "*Fine!*" and stomp off to your room. You sit in your room thinking you just can't explain anything to your parents anymore. They sit wherever they are, thinking that they hardly know who you are anymore.

These things will happen! And the sad thing is, lots of families allow these kinds of things to make them stop talking to each other about anything other than homework or when they need to pick you up at the mall.

Your open communication (talking about real stuff, life-stuff) with your parents is *so* important! Not only will it help you have a great ride through your teenage years, but it will also help you become the adult you want to be. So do everything you can—even when it's hard—to keep talking about the real stuff of life with your parents.

HONESTY

Because your brain is working in new ways now, you'll start to find out that you can get away with lying to your parents. At least sometimes you can.

But getting good at lying is a lousy way to go. First, it's totally against what God wants for us—lying is clearly a sin. But that's not just because God doesn't want you to get your way. God made that rule for a reason.

God knows (because God invented us!) that a person who starts lying to get his or her way will get good at it. But getting good at it ends up hurting you and all the people in your life more than you could ever imagine. God doesn't want us to lie because God knows being a liar will ruin your life.

And the really slippery thing about lying is: Once you start, it's super hard to stop! You won't learn how to talk about what you really want and why. You won't learn how to live with not getting your way—even when it seems unfair.

When you lie to your parents, you're really cheating yourself. You're teaching yourself what looks like a shortcut, but is really a dead end. Sure, you might get your way a few times. But you'll be giving up learning how to live a life of truth and honesty. And truth and honesty are a *huge* part of living a good life as an adult, too!

Here's the survival tip: Be totally committed to being honest with your parents. If you tell a lie, make the really hard choice of going back to them and telling them the truth. There may be a consequence for the lie—but your parents will also learn to trust you more. And in the end, you'll get *way* more freedom if you tell the truth.

NOTICING OTHER FAMILY MEMBERS' NEEDS

Picture this: You come flying in the door from a friend's house, and all you can think of doing is getting to the TV because your favorite show is just about to start. Homework's done, chores are done enough—there's nothing stopping you! You take the long way through the kitchen to grab a cold glass of milk. And there, sitting at the table, is your older brother (just substitute another family member if you don't have an older brother). He actually looks like he's been crying—and you've never seen him cry. He doesn't even respond to you entering the room. Do you:

a. Say, "Hey, crybaby! Want your baby bottle?"

b. Tiptoe through, hoping he won't say anything so you can get to your TV show?

c. Stop and ask him, gently, what's going on?

Well—we know you're not dumb, and you know the last answer is the "good" one. But, really, which is the one you would probably do?

The reality is: We *all* have needs—all the time. Some people are better at hiding them (so, for example, it might be more of a challenge to figure out what your dad's needs are). And some people have a crazy idea that having other people help them means they're weak. But most people, most of the time, really love it when people notice their needs—you sure do!

If your mom's had a long and tiring day and you still expect her to wait on you like a servant, you're not noticing her needs. If your dad has had to work around the house the last three weekends, and his need to clean out the garage for your mom's new storage plan is keeping him from the football game on TV he really wanted to watch, volunteer to help him get it done quickly!

When you notice needs people have and do what you can to meet those needs, you can make such a *huge* positive difference in your family!

INTEGRITY

If we (Kurt and Marko) tell you we're actually space aliens, we wouldn't have integrity...because, well, we're *not* space aliens.

If we tell you we're midget wrestlers from an unknown Latin American country, and we tag-team wrestle under the name "Las Floritas" (the little flowers), we wouldn't have integrity...because, well, it ain't true!

Let's say we have three pieces of wood, and we cut all three of them down the middle so you can see "the insides." The first piece, we discover, isn't wood at all. It has a Styrofoam center no different from a cheap coffee cup! And the outside is just a plastic layer made to *look* like wood! We could say this "piece of wood" has no integrity at all! It's absolutely *not* what it "says" it is.

The second piece of wood is interesting. The outside of it (called a "veneer") is actually wood. It's just really thin. And the inside is really wood, too—but it's cheap wood that's been all ground up into a pulp with glue in there to hold it all together. It looks like oatmeal made out of wood. This kind of wood is strong like real wood, but way cheaper. And this piece of wood has more integrity than the first piece (at least this one is actually made out of wood!). But it's still lacking integrity, because it's hiding something (the fact that it's not solid wood).

The third piece of wood has perfect integrity: It's solid oak, all the way through. It's exactly what it "says" it is—nothing to hide.

Do you understand "integrity" now? Honesty has a lot to do with it, but it's more than that. Integrity means doing what you say you'll do, being who you say you are, following through on commitments, and only saying what you mean (not just what you think will get you what you want). If you want your family to be the best that it can be, you *have* to be committed to living with integrity. Are you? Do you?

DOING YOUR PART

I know this part isn't fun—but it's true. If you want to have a great family, you can't assume they're all your servants!

There are a couple of normal reasons why so many young teenagers hate helping out around the house so much. First, you're going through one of the biggest times of change in your entire life. In fact, only newborn babies go through more change than you'll go through in the years between about 11 and 14. And all that change has a weird effect on most young teenagers: It makes them only see themselves.

Of course, you *see* other people—you know there are people there, living in your house. But because of all the change going on in your life and body and brain, it's easy to see yourself as the center of the entire universe—as if you're the sun, and your family (and everyone else) are the planets orbiting around bright-and-shiny *you*! This focus on yourself makes it a bit challenging to break down that orbiting thing and actually share the workload.

The other reason this is normal is that all the changes you're going through can leave you tired— really tired. Your brain is working overtime in new ways, and your body is changing and growing and stretching—and it gets worn out from all this work!

While those things are true, they don't change the fact that doing your part around the house (washing dishes, cleaning up, taking care of young siblings, taking out the trash, picking up after yourself, and so on) is something you need to share in.

Great families are a team. The team members might have different roles and responsibilities (like, part of your role is going to school, and part of the role of one or both of your parents is to work at a job that brings in money for the family to buy food and stuff). But *all* the team members have to share in "the dirty work."

Here's a survival tip: If you want your family to be great, have a great attitude when doing your jobs around the house. And try to do them without being asked (or begged!). You'll be amazed at what a difference that can make in your family—and how much it can make your own life better!

NOT-SO-RANDOM ACTS OF KINDNESS

Everyone loves nice surprises. They make us feel special, noticed, cared for, and valued.

When you do unexpected things for your parents (or your siblings), you'll blow them away. This can totally change things in your family, making an okay family pretty great, or a great family even better.

Here are some ideas:

- Leave a note in your mom or dad's briefcase that they'll find at work—one that says something you appreciate about them. You could leave this note on their pillow if they don't go to work.

- If you aren't very good at doing your chores without being asked, starting to do so can be a *huge* surprise gift to your parents.

- Offer to wash the dishes even if it isn't your job or your turn.

- Clean up a room that isn't your job to clean up. Or clean up the garage or the backyard (if you have one!).

- If you have a little brother or sister, tell your parents you'd like them to have a night out, and you'll baby-sit (without getting paid).

- Buy a small gift for a parent (or both of them, or a sibling), just to let them know you were thinking of them. Remember, it doesn't have to be expensive to be special.

FAMILY FACT: EACH FAMILY MEMBER USES APPROXIMATELY 57 SHEETS OF TOILET PAPER DAILY.

194

- Send your mom or dad an e-mail or text message, just saying, "I love you."

- Go to one of the many Web sites with free e-cards (e.g., www.hallmark.com or www.americangreetings.com) and send a free card. Again, just use this to tell them you love them, or to thank them for taking care of your lazy butt!

- Leave little sticky notes saying, "I love you," and "You're a great mom (or dad)," all over the places in your house where they spend their time (on their bedside clock, on the mirror in their bathroom, on the steering wheel in their car, and so on).

- Make something as a gift—like a picture or a craft. Giving something you took the time to think out and make for them is an extra-special surprise for most parents!

CREATING GOOD MEMORIES AND HAVING FUN!

Here's the deal: Great families have great memories. Usually those memories are of fun times you had together.

Your parents create many of the best memories you'll have as a family—like a great family vacation or a fun trip somewhere. But you play a role in these, too! You can make a family trip a nightmare or a wonderful, fun memory.

Sure, some parents *don't* offer to do things with their young teenagers very often. Sometimes that's only because they don't think you *want* to do stuff with them anymore! Try to think of something you and one of your parents both enjoy. Then suggest that you two do that thing together. Make sure it's not only something *you* enjoy doing, or it's less likely to create a great and fun memory.

Add to that: Be fun! So many young teenagers, especially as they get closer and closer to high school, get really sour and nasty. If you always have a frown on your face and never want to talk and always have a snotty response to every conversation, you'll ruin your chances of creating fun memories.

The Bible says, in Proverbs 17:22, "A cheerful heart is good medicine, but a crushed spirit dries up the bones." Be good medicine in your family, not a bone-dryer!

SECTION 17

A FEW FINAL
THOUGHTS...

(OKAY...TWO PAGES OF FINAL THOUGHTS!)

Because you spend so much time with your family, and because your family is going to be part of your life for a long, long, long time, we wanted to remind you of a few things. These are things that we've already talked about in this book, but we think they're important enough to mention one last time. Think of this final chapter as a little "cheat sheet" that you can look at whenever you need a little encouragement.

No family is perfect. Yours isn't, and ours aren't, either.

You are an important part of your family. God put you in your family for a reason. You may not always feel like it, but it's true!

Rules are good. Really, they are! Without your parents' rules, you'd probably get yourself in a whole lot of trouble. Without rules, big strong people (e.g., Marko) would steal things from little, weak people (e.g., Kurt).

Your parents care because...well, because they care. They care about your schoolwork, your choice of friends, how you spend your time, and stuff like that because they care for you, not because they're trying to ruin your life.

Siblings: If you have 'em, you gotta learn to love 'em. You didn't get to choose who you got as siblings, but you can choose how you treat them.

Blended families take extra work. If your parents are divorced or if they've recently married someone else, you're going to need to help out by sharing your feelings and sharing the load until things settle down.

Ask for help if you need it. If there are serious problems in your family, be sure to talk to your parents or somebody else you trust for help.

God is in control! No family is perfect, but God is. He has an incredible plan for you and your family.